D1411521

THE
INDOOR
GARDENER

THE INDOOR GARDENER

Creative Displays for Every Home

NOËL KINGSBURY

Photographs by Jerry Harpur

HEADLINE

First published in 1994
by HEADLINE BOOK PUBLISHING

10 9 8 7 6 5 4 3 2 1

British Library Cataloguing in Publication Data
Kingsbury, Noël
    Indoor Gardener: Creative Displays for
    Every Home
    I. Title
    653.965

ISBN 0-7472-0981-2

AN EDDISON·SADD EDITION
Edited, designed and produced by
Eddison Sadd Editions Limited
St Chad's Court, 146B King's Cross Road
London WC1X 9DH

Phototypeset in Caslon Old Face by
Servis Filmsetting Limited, Manchester, England
Origination by Global Colour, Kuala Lumpur, Malaysia
Printed and bound by Dai Nippon Printing Company,
Hong Kong

HEADLINE BOOK PUBLISHING
A division of Hodder Headline PLC
338 Euston Road
London NW1 3BH

MAGNIFICENT MEDINILLA

Page 1. *At once both exotic and blowsy,* Medenilla
magnifica *is one of the most spectacular house plants
available, a truly rewarding plant for the more experienced
indoor gardener.*

A WINDOWFUL OF COLOUR

Page 2. *Streptocarpus in a range of colours flower all
summer long in a window. (p.137)*

CONTENTS

Part One

A HISTORY OF INDOOR GARDENING

I *find the history of indoor plants an endlessly fascinating one; it is not just a story about plants but like an epic novel it is filled with strong, unforgettable characters – their perseverance, ingenuity, bravery and selflessness, but also at times their greed, arrogance, vanity and treachery. Mollycoddled in our hi-tech world, we do not realize how much the pioneers of indoor plant cultivation had to struggle with cumbersome heating equipment and inefficient glasshouses, and with plants about whose needs they knew practically nothing. Even more than the pioneer growers, the plant hunters, who actually disco- vered and collected new species, had to contend with unknown lands, peoples and floras with all their attendant mysteries, dangers, diseases and hostilities.*

Indoor plants carry with them not just stories of adventure but lessons of social and cultural history; the 'upstairs- downstairs' world of master and servant, of all-powerful head gardeners and their legions of waterers, stokers, sweepers and pot washers, and the ever-complex relationships between women and men. So when you next water your house plants, think, like I do, of all the tales they could tell.

DYNAMIC CONTRAST

Opposite. *These contrasting and strong foliage shapes form a visually exciting group in a study area in the roof space of a small city house.* (p.137)

To our distant ancestors, the growing and nurturing of house plants would have seemed strange, indeed alien. They lived with their fields and orchards, or those of their masters, in which most of them would have toiled all day to win over a precious and all too often recalcitrant harvest. Beyond their patches of keenly defended cultivation were forests, marshlands, moorlands – waste, as they termed it – full of terrors real, mythical and imagined, all too ready to claim back as its own their careful husbandry. Being surrounded, at times besieged, by vegetation, there would have been no desire to have any of it in the comparative security of the home. Only the very wealthy, and most divorced from the daily muddy realities of farming, would have welcomed the occasional decorative cut flower into the house.

Today the tables have been turned; nature lies prostrate before a worldwide industrial civilization that threatens to engulf and destroy the remains of the natural world. For many urban dwellers, the sight of a tree or a patch of grass is their daily ration of nature. The growing of house plants is one way that a little more nature can be brought into our lives, a small way to involve ourselves in the miracle of growth. Having expelled plants from so much of the earth, many people now feel the need to invite some of them back, to share the intimate space of the home.

THE BEGINNINGS UNDER GLASS
The history of house plants is inextricably tied up with the history of glasshouses, the attempts made to grow plants in climates normally too cold for them to flourish, or to produce fruit outside its natural season. The Romans had very primitive structures for the sheltering of vines and other fruit and vegetables, and the Emperor Tiberius was able to enjoy fresh cucumbers every day, thanks to the efforts of his gardener who maintained frames heated with decaying manure and covered with transparent mica crystals.

There are records of similar creations in the Middle Ages; for example the botanical gardens of Padua in Italy, the oldest in Europe, had some sort of glass structure in 1550. But it is not until the seventeenth century that attempts at sheltering tender plants became at all widespread. What might be the first record of a house plant dates from early in that century. In a volume entitled *Flores Paradisae*, Sir Hugh Platt, an inventor, suggests training vines and apricots, growing outside, into the house to ramble along the ceiling.

During the seventeenth century, there appear to have been increasing numbers of gardeners in Britain, The Netherlands and Germany building plant houses for the winter protection of myrtles, pomegranates, vines and citrus. How primitive they sound now! The basic principle was to shut the plants up behind thick rush matting blinds whenever frost threatened, hoping that the weather would relent before incarceration suffocated the plants. Towards the end of the seventeenth century, the use of heating equipment became more common, if such a term may be applied to candles and braziers, the smoke of which occasionally threatened the lives of the gardeners as much as that of the plants. The Dutch, as so often the pioneers in matters horticultural, introduced the use of cast-iron stoves with chimneys, which would at least have had the effect of reducing the dangers from smoke, if not those of baking the plants placed too close by.

The eighteenth century was the century of the orangery, large airy galleries that were basically designed to shelter the citrus trees which were so fashionable at this time. The trees spent the summer outside, being carried into the orangery for the winter. The early models had high windows along one side; later ones introduced more glass into the roof and minimized the space taken up by stonework between the windows. Always they were grand buildings that displayed confidence and social standing. Heating was usually provided by stoves, although other primitive methods remained, such as having a wheelbarrow-type device filled with burning charcoal which was pushed manually to and fro among the pots; such were the days of cheap labour.

In addition to orangeries, many wealthy gardeners had low glasshouses, termed stoves, heated with manure or tan-bark, which released

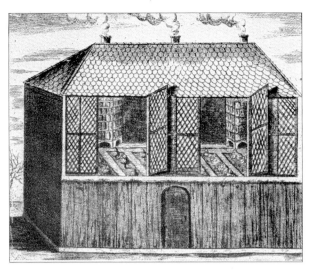

Early glasshouses such as the 1696 German pomegranate house, above, admitted only a very limited amount of light, in this case by way of leaded windows along one wall. In comparison the eighteenth-century orangery, at Mapperton in England for example, right, had larger windows and a glazed roof.

considerable quantities of heat as they decomposed. Potted plants were usually sunk in beds of the decaying material, which would supply enough heat for up to six months. Stoves were particularly favoured for the cultivation of the pineapple, something of a craze among the wealthy at this time. The presence of home-grown fruit on the dinner table was an important sign of status, and pineapples absolutely *de rigueur*.

Little else had been introduced as yet from warmer climes, and what newcomers there were were grown only by a limited number of very dedicated and wealthy people. They included cacti, passion flowers, guavas, papaya, and many species from 'New Spain', as Mexico was then known. Such plants were not grown yet for beauty's sake, but for the table, for their medicinal properties or because they excited that peculiarly eighteenth-century sense of 'curiositie'; a mixture of scientific enquiry and a naive desire to collect the unfamiliar. The growing numbers of new species being discovered at this time must have played an important part in stimulating

interest in botany, and hence assisting its development as a scientific discipline.

At around the turn of the nineteenth century, the story gathers momentum. Advances in technology made it more and more possible to build structures that enabled plants to be kept in good condition over winter. The ability to produce glass in larger quantities and sizes meant that glasshouses admitting far more light than previously could be built, which meant in turn that plants would stay healthier during the winter months. European exploration of the globe meant that increasing numbers of plants were being seen, described, desired, and then collected. It was becoming the vogue to keep plants for the sake of their beauty, not simply for utilitarian considerations. Part of this fashion involved bringing plants indoors, not at first as permanent residents, but just while they were in flower, or as temporary decoration.

The exploration of the world beyond Europe is a chapter of history in which the botanist played an often pioneering role, investigating new lands in the hunt for novel plants that might be of

Without the knowledge and labour of local people, the European plant hunters would have got nowhere, faced as they were with completely unfamiliar climates and plant life.

interest to financial backers, at first scientific but increasingly horticultural. As Richard Steele remarked in his *Essay Upon Gardening* (1793): 'To obtain these rarities men of the greatest accomplishments navigated unknown seas, have traversed drear isles and deserts, searched the forests of both the Indies and explored the burning countries of the torrid zone.'

Two of the main areas of European expansion during the latter years of the eighteenth century were the Cape region of South Africa and 'New Holland', or Australia as we now know it. The wild flowers of these lands attracted great excitement back home due to their vivid colours and the strange, even bizarre forms of some. There were, for example, heathers from South Africa with

huge sticky tubular flowers banded with pink and green, and banksias from Australia with dramatically cut leaves and enormous pincushion flower heads. Most were quite easy to grow in the unsophisticated glasshouses of the time, only needing minimal winter heating, and relishing a spell out of doors in summer.

So, after the orange, lemon and pineapple, the first real indoor plant craze was for the colourful and exotic relatives of the heathers familiar to Europeans, the Cape heaths. There are some 600 species, with flowering times spread through the year, some of the most spectacular blooming in winter. It is not surprising that the 'heathery' started to join the orangery, as an essential outbuilding for those most anxious to be in the forefront of what was becoming an increasingly exciting and fashionable hobby. Alongside the heaths were some of the lovely bulbs of the Cape, such as amaryllis and lachenalias, and the softer more opulent flowers of Mexico like daturas, *Brugmansia*, and abutilons. Some of these original introductions are still cultivated, but many, South African and Australian species in particular, are virtually never seen as glasshouse plants. Of the vast number of once popular Cape heaths, only two continue to be commercially cultivated.

With plants as fine as these, they did not stay in the functional surroundings of the glasshouse for long. They were brought inside for display, to ornament the living quarters of the house, the dining table and the ballroom, exciting the astonishment and admiration of guests. When past their best, or the great occasion was over, they were taken back to the glasshouse, where conditions were more suitable for plants. This was very much the pattern in Europe throughout the nineteenth century. There were comparatively few true house plants, more a host of temporary sojourners. The skilled head gardener and his staff were able to grow a very wide range of plants in optimum conditions under glass, taking them over to the house in their season, ensuring an ever-changing supply of beauty and novelty.

The exception to this was the conservatory. Early in the nineteenth century this term came to mean a glasshouse attached to the house, reached through doors, where there were plants growing in borders as well as in pots. An interesting record of an early conservatory is to be found in the memoirs of a French officer who appears to have lost no time in fraternizing with the local ladies on a posting to Vienna in 1803. 'It was a novel and enchanting circumstance . . . to find the apartments of most ladies adorned with conservatories and perfumed in winter with the pleasantest of flowers. I recall among others, with a kind of intoxicated delight, the boudoir of the Countess of C. whose couch was surrounded with jasmine climbing up daturas set in open soil; and all this on the first storey. You repaired from it to the sleeping chamber, through actual clusters of African Heaths, hydrangeas, camellias . . . and other precious shrubs. . . . On the opposite side was the bathroom, likewise placed in a conservatory where papyrus and iris grew around the marble basin.'

The early nineteenth century was the era of the 'gentleman amateur', men who, in the absence of scientists and engineers as we know them, experimented, designed, manufactured, promoted and bragged about an extraordinary range of glasshouse equipment. It was around this time that gardening books and journals began to be widely circulated, the journals in particular being an ideal vehicle for the wordy and excited prose of men declaiming the virtues of their particular invention, be it for heating, ventilation, glazing or watering. Some of the greatest arguments were about the glasshouses themselves; the best shape for them, the angles of the glass, the shape of the panes and even the colour of the glass. Heating systems caused much controversy, with an immense and bewildering variety of different systems being available by the mid-century, each vouchsafed as being far superior to its rivals.

Heating in the later eighteenth and early nineteenth centuries was generally carried out with fires vented out through subterranean earthenware flues, or by flues in the rear walls of lean-to structures. It was very difficult to provide a steady flow of heat (and somebody had to stay up all night to manage it), and the escape of harmful smoke and fumes was commonplace. Steam enjoyed a short vogue, either being released directly into the structure, which must have created a lot of humidity, or used to heat metal pipes. The great leap forward came when it was discovered that hot water can be made to circulate in a closed system of pipes. With this method, a simple, relatively cheap solution had been found: a boiler heated the piped water which then

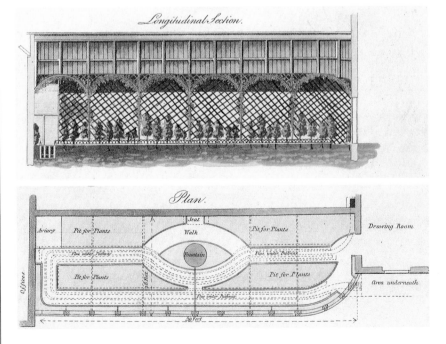

Longitudinal Section.

Plan.

The early nineteenth-century English conservatory was attached to the drawing room of the house and was heated by under-floor ducts. These conveniences allowed the viewing of plants brought in from the glasshouses to be conducted in comfortable and elegant surroundings.

circulated around the rest of the system. It provided a steady flow of gentle heat, relatively cheaply and efficiently. British inventor-gardeners bickered endlessly over who had 'invented' this system, seemingly unaware that the Russians, Germans and Austrians had for years been using hot-water heating for their 'Winter Gardens'.

THE GOLDEN AGE

Indoor gardening was now set to become one of the great obsessions of nineteenth-century Europe; the wealthy of every nation were taken up by it, but it was the British who became the most carried away. With the development of cast iron and improved methods of making glass, it became possible to build huge and fantastic structures – the Palm House in Kew Gardens in London and The Great Conservatory at Chatsworth were the two mightiest. Chatsworth was so vast it was possible to ride around inside it in a carriage. Collectors were despatched to all parts of the tropics to send back plants to their wealthy patrons, the more outrageously exotic the better. The introduction of exotics overtook that of hardy species, the gardening journals such as *The Floricultural Cabinet* and *The Botanical Register* are full of detailed descriptions of new plants, often offered for sale only a few years after their scientific description was first made. New and rare species, from orchids to fuchsias, changed hands for large sums of money, and fortunes were spent on glasshouses, equipment and staff. The possession and display of exotic plants carried great social status, and there was often considerable rivalry between wealthy growers.

It is difficult for us to comprehend the excitement that accompanied gardening in those far-off days. It seemed as if the dramatic opening up of the world to Victorian Britain and Europe had to be accompanied by some tangible sign to those back home that this 'new world' actually existed, and was not the product of some fantastic traveller's tales. The growing of plants, bizarrely different to those already familiar, may have been one way that people had to make real this whole new geographical awareness. Power had much to

do with it as well. For Europeans, and the British in particular, the world was seen as their oyster; anything they wanted was theirs. The growing of plants from far-away and dramatically different climates was a way of vaunting technological superiority and celebrating political triumph. At its best, this love of cultivating exotic beauty brought pleasure and happiness, and left behind a legacy of marvellous and elegant buildings and a considerable body of botanical knowledge. At its worst, it was an example of the greedy colonialism, so much a feature of the Victorian era.

The story of orchids illustrates the obsession for the exotic perhaps better than anything else. It also throws into sharp focus the greed and arrogance of the Victorian upper classes. Clinging to the branches of trees throughout the tropics, orchids come in a bewildering variety of shapes, sizes and colours. Their diversity and beauty appealed to the Victorians. Their collection involved great feats of hardship and frequently heroism, so that as well as buying a plant, people were buying a story and a myth, too. Rarities sold for enormous sums of money, rapidly giving them a reputation as a rich man's hobby, adding further to their already considerable mystique. The collecting of orchids could only be described as wholesale plunder; whole sections of forests were cut down, in Brazil and Colombia for example, in order to pick the plants off the upper branches; and several species were forced into virtual extinction. The plants were exported in their thousands if not millions, many dying on the journey, and the majority of the survivors failing to last more than a few years in cultivation. Sad to say, to some extent this irresponsible collecting still goes on.

Lower down the social scale, growing these exotic introductions was just as popular, but involved easier and cheaper plants, many of which are still widely grown today including begonias, chrysanthemums, petunias and, above all, pelargoniums. Many species of the latter had been first introduced in the latter years of the eighteenth century, and rapidly became popular for their ease of growth and propagation.

Australian and South African plants were among the first to be grown under glass. A few such as the epacrises and the Cape heaths remained popular until the outbreak of war in 1914.

Hybrids soon started appearing. John Claudius Loudon (1783–1843), the great gardening writer of the nineteenth century, suggested in an article in 1824 that nosegays of pelargonium flowers be suspended over one's plants so that new varieties might be created: '. . . nothing forms a more pleasing gardening amusement for the ladies of the family than saving and sowing these seeds.' It comes as no surprise that the number of pelargoniums on offer soon rocketed.

The Victorian glasshouse flora was immense, with nurseries offering a far wider range of plants for sale than is available now. Whole groups of plants that were once widely grown and loved are now virtually unknown. The bouvardias, for instance, were immensely popular in the latter quarter of the nineteenth century, especially the scented white ones which were an essential accompaniment to any middle class wedding; or the epacrises, Australian relatives of the Cape heaths, but much more tolerant of polluted city atmos-

pheres. These showy plants, with masses of richly coloured tubular flowers borne in winter, were very popular up until the First World War, but since then all the thirty or so hybrids have been lost, victims of rising energy prices and changes in fashion.

The high point of the Victorian glasshouse was the 1880s. By this time small conservatories and greenhouses were being mass produced; there were nurseries raising plants on a virtually industrial scale (three quarters of a million pelargoniums passed through Covent Garden in London in 1881) and there were numerous books and magazines to tell people what they ought to be growing, how to grow it, and where to get it from. The middle classes had arrived, anxious to proclaim and celebrate their new-found status. The possession of a glasshouse, or a conservatory even more so, was one way of displaying new-found wealth and greater standing.

The majority of plants continued to spend most of their time under glass and were only moved into the house temporarily. But an increasing number were being grown inside permanently – palms, camellias and aspidistras, for example – and for the majority of people who had neither the space or money for glass structures, this was the only way that they could enjoy exotic plants. In the United States too, far fewer people had glasshouses, partly because they were never so fashionable and also because of the severe winters on the east coast. So it was that the pioneers of the house plant were the Americans and the lower middle classes of Europe.

The Victorian home did not offer a very hospitable welcome to plant life, however. Interiors were dark and suffered violent temperature fluctuations, heated in daytime by coal fires, but allowed to get cold at night. The air too, in this the age of coal and steam, was often fearsomely polluted. The plants that could cope with this had to be real survivors – ivies and aspidistras.

There were a number of social trends and pressures that encouraged the Victorians in their persistence with growing plants in these early years. One was the idea, promulgated especially

Botany, painting – this one is by Jane Maria Bowkett – and a little gentle gardening were among the limited activities thought suitable for 'ladies' in Victorian Britain.

vigorously in the United States, notably by the writer and moralist Andrew Jackson Downing (1815–1852), that beauty and nature exerted civilizing influences, and that the presence of plants in the home would help spiritually to uplift the family. The moral aspects of gardening and botany were being promoted in Britain too, by writers like the puritanical John Ruskin (1819–1890), and they were regarded as hobbies that were specially valuable in keeping women occupied. There is little doubt that the Victorian era was a period of great social repression for the majority of women (at least in Britain); middle and upper class women were effectively banned from doing any kind of useful work, and many an active mind must have raged with boredom. Gardening, particularly indoor gardening, was a safe pastime for these suppressed energies. The irascible William Cobbett (1763–1835), writer, gardener and political campaigner, said it all in *The English Gardener* (1833): 'How much better during the long and dreary winter for daughters and even sons, to assist or attend their mother in a greenhouse than to be seated with her at cards or in the blubberings over a stupid novel or any other amusement that can possibly be conceived.'

House and conservatory plants were given far more attention than they are today, so there was plenty for bored Victorian housewives to do. Dead leaves were rigorously removed, all leaves cleaned every few days, stems assiduously tied and staked, windows opened and shut, and of course water fetched, which did not necessarily come conveniently out of a tap, but often had to be fetched from a pump. With such care and attention, it is not surprising that Victorian indoor gardeners had little problem with pests and diseases. The irony of all this activity was that a lot of women became empowered by their gardening, going on to join women's gardening clubs or working with bodies like the American Floral Missions, who distributed flowers and plants to the poor and needy.

Another irony of the Victorian promotion of gardening and botany as suitable recreations for modest ladies was the inescapable fact that flowers are the sexual organs of plants. Although taken for granted today, this fact was not widely realized until the work of Carl Linnaeus (1707–1778) was published in the eighteenth century. Linnaeus, creator of the scientific naming system upon which the classification of all living organisms is based, was a scientist, unabashed in his approach to the male and female parts of flowers. But many British writers of popular flower books were horrified at such 'immorality' and did their best to conceal any hint of sexuality in their works. In addition, there was a suspicion of flowers in certain quarters; they were seen as rather decadent, or even in bad taste, and the growing of exotic hothouse flowers came in for particular criticism from Ruskin and others. Foliage was 'chaste' in comparison, requiring the appreciation of one whose mind ran on a high moral plane. Given the problems that plants had in growing in gloomy Victorian interiors, this was just as well, few flowering plants being able to survive in such conditions.

Just as wealthier homes relied upon attendant glasshouses for a constant supply of plants, so humbler dwellings were able to enjoy seasonal flowers thanks mainly to the bulb trade. Dutch growers started marketing bulbs for flowering indoors, mainly hyacinths, narcissus and tulips, in the first half of the nineteenth century, to create what is still a major industry. Bulbs are perhaps the perfect temporary indoor plant – cheap, almost foolproof, colourful and often fragrant – and once finished with they can be planted outside. Spring bulbs rapidly became popular with all classes throughout the industrialized world, the Americans particularly. By the latter half of the century bulbs had been joined by azaleas, cyclamen and other seasonal beauties still familiar today. However, these plants were not thrown away once over, but lovingly repotted and kept out in the garden until autumn, when they would be welcomed back indoors for another season.

Another seasonal use of plants indoors was forcing hardy plants for early flower. Whereas we still force bulbs, polyanthus, and occasionally other small plants like violets and lily-of-the-valley, the Victorians regularly used shrubs like philadelphus, rhododendrons and roses, even small standard hawthorn trees. Plants would be dug up from the garden in the autumn, overwintered in containers outside and then brought into the house or conservatory for early flower and scent. Wealthy homes maintained stocks of shrubs specially for this purpose, forcing them every other year. But the practice cut across class, gardeners from cottager to Duchess seemingly used all manner of species. And for the poorer gardeners it enabled them to have plants inside without going to the expense of buying them.

So, by the late nineteenth century, there had

Plants, including a parlour palm, right, and some forced astilbes from the garden, left, take their place among the grandiloquent clutter so characteristically Victorian.

emerged a distinct house-plant flora to be found in parlours and drawing rooms across Europe and North America, tough foliage plants like aralias, dracaenas, hostas (then grown indoors), palms, and that great Victorian standby, the aspidistra. The latter's ability to cope with adverse conditions was legendary and it became such a feature of the respectable middle-class home, that in later years it found its way into the title of a novel: George Orwell's *Keep the Aspidistra Flying*, where it is used as a metaphor for bourgeois morality. Ivies too were a godsend to anyone trying to make something flourish behind the lace curtains. They were grown not only as trailers or climbing up supports, but also encouraged to attach themselves to walls – a modern interior decorator's nightmare. Not only were ivies 'chaste', but the dark greens of the leaves appealed to that sombre vein so strong in the Victorian aesthetic, the taste that initiated those dim interiors and mono-coloured men's clothing.

The aspidistra still has immensely powerful overtones of Victoriana today, and several other plants were so characteristic of the era that their presence in a room can evoke a powerful sense of period. One such is the kentia palm, *Howea forsteriana*, a plant tolerant of much neglect and abuse that became famous through its association with the 'palm court orchestras' of the late nineteenth and early twentieth century. These and other palms were even favoured as guests at dinner, tables being made with holes so that palms could rise through the centre, polite conversation carried on through the fronds.

Perhaps the pre-eminent love of the Victorians was not orchids, grown by comparatively few, but ferns. Ferns, of course, are ideally suited to growing in dark and shady places, although not many are amenable to the polluted and sometimes dry atmospheres of houses in smoky cities. An exception is the Boston fern, *Nephrolepis exaltata*, – one of several great American contributions to indoor gardening – a species that is far more tolerant of dry air, neglect, even bright light, than other ferns. It was introduced in the 1890s and rapidly became one of the most popular house plants all over the world. Previous to this, the cultivation of ferns indoors had required either careful siting and attention, or the use of a Wardian case – the fern-lovers' secret weapon.

The Wardian case was developed in the 1830s by Nathaniel Ward, a doctor and amateur naturalist working in London's East End, then as polluted an area as could be found. The case is basically a sealed miniature glasshouse, the plants inside thriving in a microclimate all of their own. It revolutionized the transport of plants on long sea journeys, making possible the introduction of yet more exotic species. It also allowed ferns and other delicate plants to be grown in places where previously only the 'cast-iron plant', the aspidistra, survived. For the remainder of the nineteenth century Wardian cases were immensely popular, made and ornamented in styles that only

The fine proportions and decorative detailing that adorned conservatories obviously inspired the maker of this Wardian case, dating from 1857, which is home to moisture-loving ferns.

the Victorians could have dreamt up; miniature temples, pagodas, replicas of famous glasshouses, some containing rockwork and elfin grottoes, collections of fossils, even a resident toad.

Tough and long-suffering botanical troopers like palms were the mainstay of the late-Victorian home, popular with anyone with the slightest social pretensions. For those with more money and space, however, the conservatory remained the pre-eminent social statement. But it also occupied a strange place in the Victorian psyche. Although the Victorians loved the sober colours that I find so drear, an aspect perhaps of their fixation with death, or their stifling social conformity, they had another side, a love of the exotic, the ornamented, the fantastical.

The conservatory was very much the place where these fantasies could be lived out. Lush greenery and rambling climbers, extravagant flowers, rockwork, pools – all were used to create a sense of being in another world, a romanticized and sanitized version of the tropics. Scent was particularly important in infusing the atmosphere of these dreamy bowers – jasmines, bouvardias, gardenias, heliotropes, tuberoses – all were used to perfume every intake of breath. The luxury and sensuousness of all of this must have been a relief from the suffocating puritanism of much of Victorian life; how much suppressed sexual energy must have gone into the making and tending of these voluptuous creations.

It is interesting to note the place that the conservatory has in the Victorian novel. It is invariably treated as somewhere apart, where the corset of social convention can be discarded, or at least loosened a little. The typical conservatory scene has lovers at a ball, making their way out of the hot and crowded house, full of prying eyes, into the relative cool and privacy of the conservatory. It is the nearest we ever get to a steamy scene in a 'respectable' nineteenth-century novel. I am particularly fond of this passage from *Not Wisely, but Too Well* by Rhoda Broughton: 'How almost oppressive, overpowering, the fragrance of the warm, damp atmosphere, where a thousand sweet smells strove perpetually for the mastery. There, side by side, gathered from the far east and the far west, blossomed and reigned Nature's most regal flower-daughters. Gorgeous stately flowers, that had hitherto revealed their passionate hearts, fold after fold, to the fainting air of some cloudless, rainless, brazen tropic sky, now poured forth all their sweets, put on all their brilliant apparel, under our watery, sickly sunbeams . . . What of man's devising can be more intoxicating than one of these temples dedicated to rich odours and brave tints? And when there stands in this temple, among these gorgeous flowers, a lovely woman . . . the subjugation of the senses may be supposed to be complete. Kate was in ecstasies.'

THE END OF AN ERA

By the late nineteenth century, the expansive self-confidence and economic prosperity of the Victorian era began to fade. In horticulture there was a renewal of interest in hardy plants, in particular those extravagantly showy rhododendrons, magnolias and other flowering shrubs being intro-

duced from the border regions of Tibet, China and Burma. And with the First World War, the death knell sounded for a whole way of life. As gardeners were sent to the killing fields of Flanders, coal was rationed, luxuries cast aside, and the crystal palaces were abandoned to their fate. Not just across Britain, but in France, Germany and other European countries boilers were turned off, watering and maintenance curtailed, and vast numbers of plants consigned to the compost heap. Symptomatic was the destruction of the great Chatsworth conservatory with dynamite in 1916.

By the 1920s the vast majority of the extensive Victorian indoor flora had disappeared; a few specimens were maintained in botanical gardens, nurseries or the glasshouses of enthusiasts. Those that remained as house plants were the toughest of the tough: *Howea forsteriana*, the redoubtable aspidistra, the rubber plant, *Ficus elastica*, a few begonias and the spotted laurel, *Aucuba japonica*, which is hardy anyway and has a remarkable ability to cope with polluted air. The more exotic plants that continued in restricted cultivation, refugees from their former popularity and surviving in a few cramped glasshouses, were often grown at somewhat lower temperatures than they had done formerly, or would do in the wild. Over the years their keepers realized how well, in fact, they grew at the more economical end of the thermometer. This knowledge was to have major implications for their reconquest of homeowners' affections in the 1950s.

There was a brief interest in cacti in the 1930s, which might have been something to do with the growing interest in abstract forms and the arrival of modern sculpture. African violet hybrids were first made during this period, but not developed on any great commercial scale. And then there was a flurry of breeding of the showy orchid cactus, *Epiphyllum* species, especially popular in Germany; each member of the Nazi leadership had one named after him. Beyond these developments, which mainly affected keen gardeners, the market for indoor plants remained static among the general public.

THE BIRTH OF THE MODERN HOUSE PLANT

With the end of the Second World War, the scene was set for major changes in all areas of life. As reconstruction progressed, and the wounds of war began to heal, people's expectations began to rise; welfare systems were instituted in some countries, helping bring to an end that fear of poverty that has haunted so many since the dawn of civilization. The comparative wealth and leisure of the Americans was now appreciated by people in Europe; here were ordinary men and women experiencing a standard of living that seemed positively luxurious compared to what they had been used to. The consumer society had begun to arrive. What were once luxuries started to become necessities.

Among the new ideas and products the Americans brought to post-war Europe was the house plant, or at least the idea that with central heating and modern lighting houses made great places for plants. The late 1940s saw a lot of experimentation with house plants in the USA, and the indoor flora that we have today is very much the product of this time. The old Victorian favourites, together with some new introductions from South America, such as philodendrons and peperomias, were carried over the threshold from the glasshouse. Most successfully of all, American growers took up the African violet, breeding new free-flowering varieties that seemed to grow perfectly in modern centrally-heated houses.

In Europe the pioneers were in Sweden, a nation whose standard of living had benefited from staying out of the war, and which was forging a new and highly influential style of interior decor, the 'Scandinavian look'. Paradoxically, the cold climate was a spur to the growing of tropical plants, as it meant that central heating was enthusiastically adopted, and it is central heating more than anything else that has made the modern house plant a reality.

With central heating, it became possible to have much more even temperatures throughout the day and night, as opposed to relying solely on open fires and stoves stoked up only when there were people in the room. In addition to central heating, post-war Swedish architects and designers were creating a style for living that was the antithesis of the Victorian: large windows, rooms with a real sense of space, furniture that was beautiful in its simplicity and purity of form. Foliage plants were brought in as design elements; climbers such as *Cissus* species were used to clothe walls, and to create screens, even borders of soil were made and plants like rubber plants and other *Ficus* species grown directly in them. In addition, Swedish architects were among the first in Europe to introduce plants into public buildings for decoration.

Designers and architects, rather than gardeners, were in the vanguard of the new boom in house plants, and given the international nature of their profession, the innovative use of plants indoors was soon spreading all over Europe,

The clean, functional look of modernism often involves the use of plants as an integral part of the design, including light lovers like this bamboo.

usually in the wake of the installation of central heating. The British, despite their love of gardens and flowers, were slow to catch on. An almost superstitious dislike of central heating and a love of opening windows, even in the coldest weather, did not lead to conditions conducive to growing house plants. It was not until the late 1950s and early 1960s that the interest in house plants really began to take off in Britain; when magazines could write of a 'vogue that is new to this generation'. By the late 1960s house plants and modern interior design had become inseparable throughout the industrialized world.

What is intriguing is just how little the range of house plants grown today has changed since the immediate post-war period, or indeed since Victorian times. Nearly all plants that are common as house plants today were current over one hundred years ago – *Ficus* species, ferns, small palms and dracaenas, for example. The only ones that our Victorian forebears would not have been familiar with are African violets, many bromeliads, peperomias and most of the philodendrons. These were introduced into widespread cultivation in North America in the late 1940s, the African violet rapidly becoming known as 'America's favourite house plant', a title it has never lost. In addition, its relatives in the gesneriad family, like streptocarpus, sinningias and gloxinias, enjoy the attentions of a large number of aficionados, even forming their own Gesneriad Society. Many amateur gardeners grow them under artificial lights, a practice the Americans refined in the early 1950s, but which has never caught on to anything like the same extent over in Europe.

Today house plants are big business, thousands of people are employed in growing, distributing, selling and caring for them and they help to create attractive living and working conditions for many millions. But the business is a cynical one; like all consumer industries it thrives on built-in obsolescence. If everyone cared for their plants so that they went on living and growing, the market would be reduced. The annual sale of millions of winter-flowering 'seasonals', like cyclamen and azaleas, is a particularly vivid illustration of this;

these plants are quite unsuited to conditions in modern houses and need care to ensure that they flower again the following year. They can live to a ripe old age, and often did with Victorian gardeners, but today's mass-produced house-plant industry is geared to rearing plants for instant and temporary effects, and the consumer is not encouraged to keep them going.

The house-plant industry is also a very conservative one; the fact that a Victorian gardener would recognize eighty-five percent of the plants, and a 1950s gardener ninety-five percent of them, does not say much for innovation or adventurousness. There is a colossal number of tropical and subtropical plants that could be grown indoors, but with the massive destruction of forests in tropical areas species of plants are being lost at a terrifying rate. As we shall see in 'A Touch of the Tropics' (pages 81 to 87), cultivation can actually save species. Unfortunately the house-plant industry seems far too complacent, and shows little interest in introducing new varieties to the trade. It is only enthusiastic amateurs and small specialist nursery owners who seem to care.

Those keen to garden indoors with a wider range of plants have to look hard to find them, but once sources are found there are great possibilities. In locating sources for the pictures for this book I discovered several small nurseries hidden away – in the Welsh mountains, in a residential street in Leeds, and in rural Devon – that supply the real indoor-gardening enthusiast. These places are worth seeking out to find plants that are just that little bit different, and a quality of personal service and advice difficult to find in the large garden centres.

At the turn of the twentieth century, lovers of house and conservatory plants had the world at their doorstep, a world full of exciting plants that could potentially grow in our living rooms today. Be adventurous, seek out and support the innovative and creative little nurseries, and the bands of amateur growers who grow unusual indoor plants. And keep your eyes open for new ideas all the time, especially when you travel abroad.

Part Two

LIVING WITH PLANTS

In selecting the photographs for this book, I wanted to show how plants can be used imaginatively and artistically around the home. I was particularly keen to find examples of plants that have been looked after for many years, thrived and become an integral part of their surroundings. I also sought to include more unusual indoor plants; not difficult or rare, but those that the house plant industry does not sell. In this I have been helped immensely by several small nurseries and growers who sell plants that are just a little bit different, brothers and sisters of mass-produced species in many cases. To anyone who wants to be a little adventurous, these nurseries are wonderful places to visit with infinitely more character and interest than any garden centre; and their owners have an unrivalled knowledge of the plants they grow, which they are only too happy to share.

The home provides a variety of plant habitats – from bright and sunny to gloomy and cold. Explore them with me, and deck them to advantage with climbers, trailers, bromeliads, orchids and other tropical plants.

MAKING THE MOST OF THE SUN

Opposite. *A varied collection of plants placed in and around an old cot make the most of the light from a sunny window. Those less tolerant of direct sunlight are placed in the shade of the sunlovers.* (p.138)

Living with plants involves sharing your home not only with inanimate objects like pictures or ornaments or pieces of furniture, but with organisms that need air, water and food just like ourselves. Therefore before starting to introduce plants into your home it is very important to understand what this means. Many people fail with house plants, even very skilled outdoor gardeners, because they underestimate the dependency of house plants and the extent to which these plants rely on their owners for the fulfilment of their every need.

Nowadays it is so easy to buy any number of items with which to improve or beautify our homes, and there are no end of magazines and books that suggest ideas for such purchases; the choice of curtains, furniture, lighting and ornaments is quite staggering. Fashion is no longer quite the dictator it once was, and any one of a variety of 'looks' can be equally up to date. If you are worried a style might not be up to the minute, then you can simply say 'It's period!' Whether

your taste is for high-tech industrial, Victorian, 1960s Scandinavian, olde-English farmhouse, ethnic, colonial or a post-modernist idiosyncratic style all of your very own, there is no shortage of shops and markets to scour in the search for whatever is appropriate. Among all these accessories are plants – another range of ornaments to help you create a particular ambience.

But plants are not like vases or tiles or chairs. The latter may gather dust if left alone, or at the worst fade, but they won't die. A house plant, unlike a garden plant, is totally dependent on you for water and feeding. It is also dependent on you finding it the right place. Every type of plant has a preference for a particular environment; just as we are comfortable and can function effectively only within a particular temperature range and in certain light conditions, then so can plants. Your house plants will fail unless you understand and are sensitive to their particular needs.

Living with plants involves first of all selecting the appropriate plants for your home. What

FORM AND FRAGRANCE

A number of unusual indoor plants occupy a corner of a modern apartment. The tall ginger lily, Hedychium, *which has deliciously fragrant, white flowers, has plenty of 'presence' with the added advantage of taking up little space. (p.138)*

TABLETOP TREE

A bonsai captures the spirit of a full-sized tree, but in miniature. Although bonsai are capable of reaching an advanced age, several hundred years in some cases, with careful training and pruning they can look venerably old even when quite young. (p.138)

often happens is that someone sees a plant they like in a garden centre or shop, thinks, 'Oh! That will look lovely in the hall'; they buy it and find out too late that it needs good light and high temperatures, and the hall is dark and cold. Present buying can add embarrassment to failure; buying something for grandad's hall that dies in two weeks will make all concerned feel sad. Selecting the right plant is not made easier by the often inadequate labels. Multinational retailing often means that labels bear only scant cultural information in as many languages as can be fitted onto a small piece of plastic. Even worse are the tiny symbols with no words of explanation at all. Unfortunately garden centre staff are often inadequately trained to deal with enquiries.

Reading this book will give you a much clearer idea of what kind of plants do well in different parts of the home, and there are several excellent and cheap A to Z house plant guides available. Take one with you when you go plant shopping for it will save much heartache.

I think the two key words in growing plants successfully are 'sensitivity' and 'compromise'. Sensitivity to the needs of the plants in your care and compromise because there is a certain amount of give and take involved in growing indoor plants. This is, admittedly, a bit one-sided because it is, after all, your home and the plants are for your enjoyment and benefit. But you do have to give a little, perhaps by accepting that you cannot always have plants exactly where you want them. For instance, maybe only an ivy will grow in the cold dark hall which, ideally, you would like to fill with orchids. You may also need to change the conditions somewhat if plants are to thrive, for example, by increasing the humidity in a warm room. The really dedicated grower of indoor plants may want to compromise further in giving over living space to particularly valued plants. Personally speaking, I would like to live in a large glasshouse, with furniture scattered amongst verdant tropical growth – but this is probably an uncommon fantasy!

Plants that share your living space do have to compromise however, because a plant living in a house is very rarely growing in the kind of conditions it would in the wild, or even in a garden or glasshouse. Light is so often a limiting factor. Indeed I am somewhat notorious for my refrain of 'not enough light' when asked to diagnose the problems of my friends' indoor plants. Many plants are grown indoors in light conditions consistently lower than they would live in naturally. This is not necessarily a problem as we shall see in the section dealing with growing in the shade, for many plants will continue to be attractive and healthy in places that would be too dark for them in their natural environment. Conditions in most houses are cooler and less humid than those required by many of the tropical plants that we grow, and yet these plants will survive and stay healthy, only growing a lot more slowly than they would do normally. Think about this in human terms. What is it like for people from temperate climates when they visit the tropics? They are perfectly able to function, but at reduced efficiency. You need to be aware that many of the plants in your home are growing in less than ideal conditions, and sensitivity to this fact can make you a much better indoor gardener. For example, a maidenhair fern in a hall window is probably having to put up with much drier air than it would prefer. Being aware of this, the good grower will mist it occasionally, stand it on a saucer of wet gravel or just keep an eye open for tell-tale signs of trouble, such as yellowing fronds or brown tips.

POEM IN BROWN AND BLUE

An unusual arrangement of feathers, dried flowers and minerals incorporates a jewel orchid, named for its exquisite leaf markings. These natives of China and Southeast Asia are the only orchids grown for their leaves rather than their flowers. (p.138)

STAIRWAY AND SUNSET

The last beam of the evening sun strikes a small statue of Icarus and some plants on a stairway. The cardamon, centre, has leaves that release a delicious spicy fragrance when rubbed; it is a remarkably tolerant and easy plant. (p.138)

It is best to start off by buying top quality plants. Avoid those greengrocers, hardware shops and garages that stand plants outside to brave all weathers. Garden centres are usually the best places from which to buy plants as they usually have good quality, carefully selected stock. Look to see there are no obvious signs of pests or disease, that the stems are well clothed with leaves and there is fresh growth, such as new leaves unfolding. Flowering plants should have lots of buds. Avoid compost that appears soggy and slimy as it may mean that the plant has been overwatered and could be suffering root rot. The other danger sign is where compost has shrunken away from the side of the pot; a result of drought, the compost can be difficult to re-wet.

Many new plant owners worry that a slight chill will do great damage to a new plant on the way home. In fact, with the exception of a few highly strung subjects like caladiums, an hour or two of cold air (not sub-zero though!) won't do any harm; however, overheated car interiors can. Once home a new plant should be kept out of bright sun for a few weeks; be prepared to accept the occasional dead leaf or aborted flowers as the plant adjusts to its new home. If all appears well after about two weeks, then the plant can be placed in its permanent abode. Seasonal and temporary flowering plants like chrysanthemums and cyclamen should be placed in their new quarters straight away, which usually means a good light and fairly cool position. Also remember that just as the plants enhance your living space so do the planters, pots or trough in which they are stood. They should harmonize with your decor or be quietly unobtrusive.

Once you have got your plants safely home and they have adjusted to the conditions in your home, you can put them on display. This is one of the most enjoyable aspects of indoor gardening. So whatever the conditions you offer your plants – whether they bask in the sun or green up the gloom, whether the heat is on or off – join me in the following pages of this book where I shall be looking at how house plants can be used adventurously and imaginatively around the home.

GROWING TOGETHER
Indoor plants in groups

I s it best to grow plants in groups or on their own? As far as the plants are concerned, they are much happier in groups. Together they can create their own microclimate to some extent, building up an island of slightly higher humidity than that in the room around them. If you think about it, plants mostly grow together in the wild. How often do you see a plant growing naturally all on its own, like one of those cartoons of a desert island with a single palm tree? As far as you are concerned, one well-placed group will have a lot more impact than individual plants scattered all around a room. A solitary plant can be highly effective as a so-called specimen plant, but on the whole groups work best for plants and for people.

From a practical point of view, it is much easier to care for a group of plants than a scattered collection; there is less running around with the watering can, for example. From a plant designer's angle, there is greater scope for creating interesting and attractive effects using several plants near each other. Small plants with small leaves, like some of the pileas, peperomias or cacti, can get a bit lost on their own. However, used in a group they can actually become more important visually.

PICK OF THE BEST

A Victorian-style cast-iron plant stand is ideal for the temporary display of plants when they're looking at their best. It is also an excellent means of saving space. (p.138)

One very good reason to think in terms of plant groupings is the eminently practical one of hiding any unattractive features; for example, small leafy plants can be positioned to mask the bare stems of taller subjects. We expect so much of our house plants, including that they will be perfect when viewed on their own. Garden centres must take much of the blame for this, with their unreasonable demand that all their plants should look as if they are going to win first prize, staged in splendid isolation, at a village flower show. In reality most plants that look great in a border are disappointing in a pot. The lanky bare stems, floppy branches and untidy new growth sprouting out at odd angles are all too apparent. Although there are house plants, palms for instance, which will always look very respectable on their own, there are many more that won't, even with the best care in the world. Dieffenbachias and codiaeums for instance have wonderful, richly coloured foliage but all too often this is absent from their lower stems, giving them a bare leggy appearance. Grouping plants is therefore not only more natural and practical, but more realistic too.

Where in the house should plant groupings go? Most people like to have their best plants in the living room, clearly on show to family and friends. Consequently these groups need to look good for as much of the year as possible. To keep up appearances it might even be worth moving plants around between rooms, with the best ones always on display where they are most important visually. Bear in mind though that the living

SHADES OF PURPLE

The afternoon sun lights up three plants with contrasting foliage shapes but similar purple or dark colouring. The Begonia rex *on the left will look even more lovely when lit from behind.* (p. 139)

room is usually the warmest room in the house, and often has the driest atmosphere – not congenial for many plants. This is all the more reason for having a generous-sized grouping; not only will the plants create a slightly more humid microclimate for themselves, but it will be easier to provide it for them by placing the pots in a tray filled with damp gravel.

Kitchens and bathrooms are often the best rooms in the house for plants, especially those originating in the tropics, because of the combination of a warm temperature and high humidity. Even a cold bathroom can be a haven for an appropriate selection of ferns. The space for plant groupings can be limited however, especially in the kitchen. Beware of confusing your plants with those for culinary use – I have accidentally included house plant leaves in salads! The kitchen windowsill, however, is a classic home for plants. This situation frequently provides a good combination of warmth, humidity and light, and plants

so placed tend to get looked at more frequently. It is the ideal place for cuttings and seedlings, and sick plants that need tending will get examined every time you do the washing up.

Halls and passageways are often cramped, but if there is space and reasonably good light they offer a lot of scope. An arresting display of plants in the hallway immediately creates a favourable impression on visitors. Halls often include stairs and thus open up the possibility of extending growing space vertically to provide a place for a tall tree like a weeping fig, *Ficus benjamina*, or palm, or a climber such as a philodendron or cissus. Any of these could be complemented by other plants at the base or placed at strategic intervals up the stairs or on a landing.

Bedrooms are rather underrated as places for house plants – a shame as they can offer great possibilities. Think about going to sleep, or making love, surrounded by exotic foliage and romantic flowers. My all-time favourite bedroom flowers are those tropical plants which release their scent only at night, such as night-scented jessamines, *Cestrum nocturnum*. Needing plenty of light, they are best grown in the conservatory and brought in when they are in flower. Bedrooms are often spacious so why not use this space to good effect with a carefully selected plant grouping? Relaxing, muted colours and soft outlines are more appropriate for the bedroom than bold forms. Bedrooms tend to be colder than other rooms in the house, which may rule out implementing the wilder flights of tropical fancy. However, the cool temperatures can make them suitable for many plants including cyclamen and azaleas, or abutilons and scented winter jasmine, *Jasminum polyanthum*.

The indoor gardener can really go to town with plant groupings in the conservatory or garden room. Displays of flowers can be changed seasonally. Even in the smallest conservatory there is space in the corners or along a wall that can be filled with pots of colourful plants.

The creation of a successful grouping is the art of compromise between what looks good artistically and what will work horticulturally. For example, it is no good putting together succulents and ferns and expecting them to live happily ever after. The contrasting leaves and stems may look great, but the two groups of plants have completely different needs. The succulents require strong light while the ferns prefer shade and humidity.

Of course there is nothing stopping you from creating culturally incompatible groupings for a limited period. For example, many people who keep succulents outside on a terrace in summer bring them in over the winter, during which time they grow very little, and can make do with much less light than during their period of active growth. This means that in the winter months succulents could cohabit with ferns or other shade lovers so long as they are separated and despatched to appropriate homes once growth starts.

Should groups of plants be grown together in one container, or should they be in separate ones? My feeling is very much that each plant should be in its own pot. Plants whose roots all share a common container will inevitably compete for moisture and nutrients, with one or two fast-growing bullies taking over at the expense of the others. Keeping plants in their own pots makes it possible to remove them easily if they deteriorate or if you want to change them around. You may like the idea of an 'indoor garden', where all the plants are apparently growing in soil. In this case you can always sink individual pots in a large container of compost or chipped bark to create the illusion that they are growing happily together.

Plant groups, then, don't have to be permanent; it is much more fun and stimulating to have groups that are constantly changing. Some plants benefit from being moved around with the seasons; others, like flowering bulbs and cyclamen, will only be worth displaying for a limited period. You may want to move plants around to see how well they do in different places, to experiment with different combinations of colour, form and texture, or just because you get bored easily. Changing plants around is a good opportunity for some gardening. So before you put your plants in their new positions check for

A CORNER OF ELEGANCE

Three of the plants have hand-shaped, or palmate, leaves, which provides a unifying theme. An alcove can make a most attractive place in which to display plants, but the plant group must be of suitable proportion. (p.139)

pests and diseases, tidy up dead leaves, repot or feed with a long-life fertilizer. Most plants have no objections to being moved, so long as the new conditions are not too different from the old. Particular care needs to be taken when moving from warm to cool, or from low light to high, and a period of adjustment in a 'halfway house' is a good idea in such circumstances.

Plants that are intended to live together permanently will need to have compatible requirements. The best way to plan such combinations is to decide on the location and then to browse through an A to Z guide, making a list of all the plants that will grow in the given conditions. Then think about which plants on the list will look good together and are readily available.

Take the example of a landing at the top of the stairs with an empty corner which you think could benefit from some plants. There is quite a bit of height, so a floor-based display including at least one tall plant would look rather good. It is warm, a minimum of 15C (60F), as heat rises up the stairs, but it never feels hot and stuffy so the air should not be too dry. There isn't too much light, however, certainly no direct sunlight, but neither is it dark. Skimming through a table of cultural conditions will produce a list of plants that could include the following: *Aglaonema*, *Anthurium*, *Asplenium*, *Crossandra*, *Calathea*, *Dichorisandra*, *Spathiphyllum*. Reading through the individual entries reveals that *Crossandra* have a reputation for being difficult, so you decide against them. *Dichorisandra* sounds good especially since it grows quite tall, but your local garden centre hasn't had one in for years. Which leaves you with a selection whose leaf form tends to be fairly similar and whose colours are inclined to be rather dark. *Aglaonema* and *Calathea* are available in attractively coloured forms, but they are not quite enough to 'lighten' the selection. In addition, none of these plants give any height.

Now you will need to look for plants which tolerate a lower minimum temperature, say 10C (50F), but are happy to grow at temperatures above this. Another trawl through your A to Z guide will turn up various possibilities. Among them could well be two ferns, which will not mind the relatively low light levels and will contribute dramatically different leaf form and colour: the arching blue-green fronds of *Polypodium aureum* and the formal 'vase' of the pale green bird's nest fern, *Asplenium nidus*. As for taller plants, your second list could well include two palms – *Howea forsteriana* and *Rhapis excelsa* – both of which grow quite tall and are tolerant of a wide range of temperatures and varying levels of humidity and light.

Before you start to plan your plant group you should consider the overall effect you want to create, and how it will relate to the room as a whole. Plants can affect their surroundings in different ways, and the converse is true too.

First of all I want to consider how the room affects the plants. The background can make a lot of difference as to how well the plants are seen. A complex and intricately patterned wallpaper is no good as a background for plants with small leaves, as they will tend to 'disappear' or look annoyingly fussy. Better to go for bold shapes, like monstera, large-leaved philodendrons or broad-foliaged palms like *Howea*. However, large-leaved plants may create too many exciting contrasts in front of a bold-patterned wallpaper, and leave the poor viewer somewhat over-stimulated. What you can do though, is to create 'echoes'. For example, a chunky, abstract painting can be echoed by a simple and bold plant standing nearby, such as one of the banana family – a *Musa* or *Strelitzia*.

The same applies to colours; pale or variegated leaves, or pastel flowers may be swallowed up by a subtle-coloured background, and dark leaves by a dark background. But echoing can also work with colours, as can be seen if a yellow and red croton, or *Codiaeum*, is placed within a few metres of a painting of a sunset, for instance. Pale colours can be used to light up a dark corner, and dark foliage to give contrast and depth to a light room. Colours affect mood too. Dark leaves can be quite funereal; reds and yellows are 'hot'; blue-greens cooling, and mid green helps create a lush spring-like ambience.

Just as plant colours can affect the atmosphere of a room, so can their shapes. Small hairy plants like African violets are almost like pets, giving a

A LIVELY BUNCH

A sunny corner of a well-lit room is home to a number of plants whose variety of contrasting leaf shapes and colours is lively and stimulating. Note how the pots are placed at different heights.
(p.139)

feeling of cosiness and homeliness. Dramatic forms like large-leaved palms, sansevieras, dracaenas, ponytail palms – *Beaucarnea recurvata* – and alocasias produce an atmosphere of dynamic energy and hi-tech modernity, even more so if very different leaf shapes are combined. Spiny forms of cacti, yuccas and above all agaves, can feel quite aggressive, even if you don't actually touch them.

Ambience is often affected by cultural associations. Bamboos instantly evoke the Far East, citrus remind one of the sunny countries where they grow, aspidistras almost always conjure up the Victorian era whilst howea palms suggest turn-of-the-century ballrooms.

Lighting can affect the appearance of plants. Some plants are best back-lit, others should be lit from the front. *Kohleria* 'Dark Velvet' is a good example of the former; its dull reddish leaves glow when lit from behind. *Anthurium crystallinum*, however, only comes into its own when light falls on the upper surface of its large heart-shaped leaves, making visible the shining white lines formed by the veins that cross the surface. Shadows, too, are important. Palms in particular throw wonderful shapes across the wall and the ceiling if the light comes from the right angle. Don't be afraid to spend some time experimenting. Move your plants and artificial light sources around to achieve the most pleasing effects.

Grouping indoor plants not only benefits the plants, but offers endless possibilities to the creative imagination. Be adventurous, and don't be afraid to move your plants around if the first attempt does not work, or you fancy a change. The good gardener and designer is always willing to try something different.

COOL AND CLASSICAL

These plants have been selected for their grey marked leaves which consort well with the trellis on the wall behind. The pink flamingo flower, Anthurium, *provides a delicate spot of contrast.* (p. 139)

CONTRASTING THREESOME

Opposite. *A simple group of three, with contrasts in leaf size, shape and colour – vibrant in the case of coleus. A larger group with such contrasts could* *prove too restless to the eye. It is worth noting that odd numbered groups are more pleasing than those with even numbers.* *(p.139)*

VARIETY AND BALANCE

Above. *Supported at a variety of heights these plants wrap round a corner. Despite their widely differing leaf shapes and colours, the plants are similar in outline which helps to keep the* *group visually pleasing. The* Cissus rhombifolia, *far right, sometimes known as grape ivy, is normally grown as a climber, but here makes an effective trailer.* *(p.140)*

Once a Warehouse

Left. *This corner of a converted store has been transformed by an elegant selection of plants. The scindapsus, growing far left, is an easy-going and adaptable* plant, *equally at home as a climber or as a trailer. The tall ming aralia has an imposing but attractive tree-like habit. (p.140)*

Winter Scene

Above. *The variegated farfugiums, placed at the front, have been brought inside for the winter to join two cycads — slow-growing, primitive palm-like plants. A mistletoe fig, to the right, named for its white, winter berries, completes this group of interesting foliage plants. (p.140)*

BASKING IN THE SUN
Plants for bright light

Sunlight streaming in through the windows dispels gloom and lifts the spirits, especially in the darker days of winter. The sun's warming rays can seem like an invitation to sit down and relax. Such a sunny site might be the obvious place to put plants, indeed it can be, but they need choosing carefully. Some plants like to bask in the sun, to have as much light as you can give them, but others dislike too much and are easily damaged by it. Many house plants have been selected as suitable to share our lives precisely because they do not need full sunlight, growing naturally in forests, in dappled shade where they receive only filtered light. Plants for a really bright sunny room will often be species that are native to open country, maybe arid for much of the year, with little or no shading from trees.

Many of the most rewarding flowering indoor plants – jasmines, abutilons, bougainvilleas and pelargoniums – need good light. They tend to be fast growers and require high light levels to produce the healthy new growth that will carry the buds for the next crop of flowers. In places where there is no direct sunlight, such plants will grow spindly and weak and no flower buds will

form. On the whole, these kind of plants do best in a conservatory, but if you do have a very sunny window, a bay window in particular, then they can give good results.

In this section we will look at those plants that thrive in direct sunlight for at least half the day, and relish it all day long. We must not forget how much energy the sun's rays carry. Those picture or bay windows that are ideal winter sun traps can make a room feel like the Sahara Desert on a summer's day, especially if you have neglected to leave the windows open. Plants can dry out and wilt distressingly fast in such conditions. Often these sun traps are places that are very important in the home, living and dining rooms are often built to face the sun, and they are the places where we most want to see plants. Thriving plants too, not specimens with the brown-edged leaves and bare stems that show that they have dried out once too often.

Succulents and other desert plants are the ideal solution for the place that is liable to get very hot, particularly if watering is likely to be erratic. Succulents and cacti are extraordinarily sculptural plants, with an amazing variety of shapes, sizes and textures. There are the column like cereus cacti and the very similar but totally unrelated African euphorbias; the rounded, almost spherical forms of mammillaria and rebutia cacti; the assemblages of plate-like stems of the opuntias; the rosettes of aloes, echeverias and agaves. If you want to create a dynamic, spiky, almost aggressive display of plants then there is endless scope here. The range of form to experiment with

A BOLD STATEMENT

The palm Archontophoenix cunninghamiana *makes a bold statement in a well-lit living room. Although its size might overwhelm a smaller space, here its height is in scale and its central position in the room makes a focus of interest.* (p.140)

exceeds the wildest imaginings of the most avant-garde of abstract sculptors. Even leaving aside the more fearsomely spiky agaves and cacti, the dramatic contrasts that can be achieved by mixing different succulents together can create an exciting, constantly stimulating, almost restive feature.

Not everyone likes the drama of the bolder succulents, finding them too hard and aggressive. But there are plenty that have a softer feel — echeverias, for instance, which form neat rosettes of glaucous foliage and freely produce colourful orangey flowers. Some succulents have a habit resembling a miniature tree, such as *Crassula argentea*, easily grown into an impressive, almost bonsai-like, specimen plant. Then there are many cacti whose rounded shapes make them appear cuddly, rather than dynamic and thrusting. In addition, many of these smaller cacti — mammillarias, rebutias, parodias — flower spectacularly in early summer, in shades of red, pink, orange and yellow. A few succulents are grown for their flowers rather than their foliage, rocheas and kalanchoes for instance, and their cheerful colours can do much to enhance a sunny windowsill.

These smaller succulents are the ideal plants to grow on a hot sunny windowsill, and a surprisingly large collection can be fitted into a small space. Windowsills that are hot during the day can get surprisingly cold at night, especially if the curtains are drawn, but succulents, being desert plants, are used to this. The enthusiastic grower of succulents may well want to increase the capacity of these hot spots by building in extra shelves across, or by suspending trailers from the top and sides of the window recess.

Palms often associate well with succulents, especially those with hard dramatic foliage, like the date palms, *Phoenix*. These palms will grow well, too, in conditions of strong sunlight, and can provide the height and lightness of touch that are more difficult to achieve with succulents alone. Although not true desert plants, palms are associated in our minds so much with deserts that they can be used with succulents to help create the hot dry ambience of an adventurous place.

There are other tall-growing plants suitable for bright sunny spaces, yuccas and cordylines for instance. They live naturally in semi-arid environments and are thus used to direct sunlight and seasonal drought. Their ease of growth, and their tolerance of neglect and a wide range of conditions has resulted in their becoming very popular as indoor plants.

Plants that are sold for their flowers often need conditions of bright light. Indeed it can be difficult to provide sufficient light in the home for them to carry on flowering as profusely as when they were bought. A very sunny window can be a suitable home, however, especially if there is no risk of their watering needs, which may be daily

SOAKING UP THE SUN

This bright room with its sunny bay window is ideal for a variety of mostly desert plants: yucca, sansevieria, cacti and other succulents. The range of sculptural forms taken by succulents is remarkable and very decorative. (p.140)

Miniature cyclamen and mixed kalanchoes are used to add winter colour to a more permanent collection of foliage plants in this bedroom. Such flowering plants almost invariably need a great deal of light. (p.141)

in summer, being neglected. Many abutilons, bougainvilleas, passion flowers, or *Passiflora*, and daturas, or *Brugmansia*, grow quite large and will need frequent and careful pruning if they are not to take over the window completely. Fuchsias flower well outside during the summer months, and this is really the best place for them, bringing them in before the frosts to enjoy the last flowers of the season inside. Marguerites, or *Argyranthemum*, and pelargoniums can be treated in the same way, although these can often flower well into the winter. Indeed the ordinary common zonal pelargonium or bedding geranium is, I think, one of the best indoor flowering plants for the winter. If found a cool light window it will be in bloom all through the colder months.

In winter, light levels are much lower than in summer, and a sunny window becomes a more amenable place for a wider range of plants. Species that normally dislike too much direct sun, such as begonias and bromeliads, will benefit from being moved to a brighter place at this time

of year. Winter-flowering pot plants need good light as well, but should be moved to a shadier position towards the end of their season, as temperatures and the fatal risk of drying out both rise. Such plants do best if they can be kept light and cool.

Of the smaller flowering house plants, like African violets and streptocarpus, many will be rapidly baked in a sunny window, but there are some that will cope. The Madagascar periwinkle *Catharanthus roseus* and busy lizzies, *Impatiens*, are two that will. In some cases leaves can be as colourful as any flower; witness the incredible range among coleus. Needless to say, all these non-succulents must be watered regularly.

So, when choosing plants for the sunniest windows in the house, beware, for like a desert mirage it is not all it seems and can be a very inhospitable place. If there is any doubt that you will not be able to keep up the pace with the watering can, make sure that you choose those plants that can take the heat and the drought.

PLANTS FOR MODERN LIVING

Left. *Large foliage plants enhance a stylishly modern apartment: they introduce a note of softness and life in a room that might otherwise be rather stark. The arching branches of the rubber tree are most effective in this respect. (p.141)*

IMPRESSIVE SPECIMENS

Above. *A large open room, like this one in a converted factory, needs plants with stature, such as the venerable dracaena to the left and the hibiscus trained as a standard. The white-painted walls create a very reflective and light, but not dazzling, environment. (p.141)*

AN AUTUMN RARITY

Opposite. *Surrounded by small succulents is the Scarborough lily, a bulb that flowers in late summer and autumn. Very* popular a hundred years ago, it is now rarely seen, which is unfortunate as it is reliable and needs little care. (p.142)

PLANTS AND MASKS

Above. *A number of light-loving and very sculptural plants are displayed with a collection of South American figurines and masks. The dracaena, on the right, and screw pine, by the window, both make easy specimen plants which are suitable for most home conditions.* (p.141)

DESERT FISH

Left. *Painted model fish keep company with several miniature cacti in an unusual and witty use of a glass goldfish bowl. Naturally small and slow-growing species have been chosen and such a planting should be watered with great care during the summer months.* (p.142)

A Tree Indoors

Left. *Texas ebony makes an attractive specimen tree in this well-lit corner of an artist's home. Its gift is to combine substantial size with airy lightness. (p. 142)*

Spikes and Curves

Above. *Two spiky succulent sansevierias contrast well with the rounded shapes of the large earthenware bowl and the swollen, water-storing trunk of a ponytail palm. (p. 142)*

COLOUR IN THE LEAVES

Left. The familiar rubber plant alongside one of its lesser-known relatives, Ficus rubiginosa *'Variegata', and a cordyline. As with other variegated plants they all need good light to maintain brightly coloured leaves. Take care when putting variegated plants together as too many can look fussy. (p.142)*

DEGREES OF LIGHT

Above. This picture illustrates well how light levels change around a window. The pink-flowered pelargonium needs and will receive the most direct sun. The Cissus rhombifolia *next to it gets the sun every morning, while on the table a syngonium and a flowering rechsteineria receive the good but indirect light they prefer. (p.142)*

SWOLLEN STEMS OF THE DESERT

Opposite. *Some desert dwellers, such as the pachypodiums and the bowiea here, have developed thickened stems rather than* *succulent leaves to conserve water, which, although they may not be everyone's idea of beauty, have a curious charm. (p.143)*

SUCCULENTS *EN* MASSE

Above. *This pot planted with a selection of succulents illustrates well the wide variety of form, colour and habit that they have.* *The contrast between those with dark leaves and those with grey foliage is especially dramatic. (p.142)*

LIGHT BUT NOT BRIGHT
Soft and subdued light

Much of the space in our homes is light, but does not receive much, if any, direct sunlight. The majority of house plants have been selected to suit this indirect light. Windows that do not directly face the sun will only get sunlight for a few hours a day, while those that face away from it may not get any, but still have a good quality soft light. It is these situations that are the best in which to grow indoor plants – plenty of light for healthy growth but not so much that they get baked dry every time the sun shines.

Lack of light is perhaps the greatest limitation on what can be grown indoors. It is a difficult problem for us to appreciate as our eyes have an ability to adjust to light which prevents us from judging accurately its intensity. Plants, in contrast, are very sensitive to light, their whole metabolism being dependent on its strength. Too little light, and growth is spindly and anaemic looking, while too much means many plants suffer from bleached and scorched foliage. Once we can appreciate the sort of light plants need, we can achieve much better results.

So where in the home is light but not bright? Rooms that face the sun and have plenty of large windows, where only real light lovers will thrive

VARIEGATED BEAUTY

This form of Ficus aspera *is one of the most attractive of all variegated-leaved plants for the home. Here it enjoys good but indirect light from a window to the right. (p.143)*

near the glass, will have more suitable conditions for plants requiring good but indirect light further back, perhaps as far as the rear wall. Rooms that receive only a few hours direct sunlight a day will have suitable positions near the windows, and maybe as far back as the middle of the room. Those rooms that never see the sun can offer a good home on the windowsill, but not much further back. Of course, window size makes a great deal of difference, and those of us who live in older houses with small windows are much more limited, as less light penetrates the room than in most modern houses. Skylights should not be forgotten, indeed for the plants described in this chapter they can offer an excellent source of high quality indirect light.

The colour of the walls also affects light intensity. White-painted or pale walls reflect light so making a room a brighter place for plants. Fluorescent lighting is a good supplementary light source for plants, unlike conventional tungsten lighting, although if you are seriously interested in growing under artificial light it is worth buying lighting tubes that are specially designed to encourage plant growth.

In this section, I will look first at flowering plants for subdued light, then at foliage plants with brightly coloured foliage, and finally at those species which impress with their form, style or elegance, rather than with their colour. What most of these plants have in common is that in the wild they live in woodland – not great dark forests, but lighter more open woods where they receive dappled sunlight or half shade.

The gesneriads are first and foremost among those families that have provided us with good house plants, a truly wonderful source of colourful and amenable varieties. The African violet is one example, so are the gloxinias, *Sinningia*, and the streptocarpus. Most gesneriads are compact, with rounded and hairy leaves that give them an endearing furry animal-like quality which must contribute greatly to their appeal. African violets were first hybridized in Germany in the 1920s, crossing the Atlantic to become 'America's favourite house plant' by the late 1940s. Now they are available in an enormous variety of shapes, sizes and colours – from white to deepest imperial purple and intense dark blue, and in various shades of pink. There are examples with variegated foliage, trailing habits, miniatures, and others with crinkly or double flowers. They are the ideal plant for a small windowsill which gets good light but little direct sun, and for someone who is not too generous with the watering can. Remember that they come from seasonally dry areas of southern Africa where they are never constantly moist. The irony is that the wild species are now in danger of extinction through habitat destruction, and no one seems to care.

African violets are jewel-like in their compactness and intensity of colour, whereas their larger relatives the gloxinias (more properly hybrids and cultivars of *Sinningia speciosa*) appear more like cheap and cheerful ornaments from the market. Larger and gaudier, the latter have a shorter flowering season and a strictly seasonal habit, dying down after flowering to tubers which need to be kept dry and dormant until the following spring. Sharing this seasonal habit are several other members of the same family, such as kohlerias, which have charmingly spotted flowers, and achimenes, irrepressibly jolly plants with pansy-shaped flowers popular with the Victorians, but now enjoying a modest revival thanks to renewed breeding programmes in the United States. Achimenes come in violets, reds, pinks and whites and flower for several months in the summer. The trailing habit of many make them good hanging basket plants.

There is definitely something addictive about growing gesneriads, there is even a Gesneriad Society in North America. One man who has made a hobby of collecting them into a successful business is Rex Dibley, a former school biology teacher. He now, with the help of his family, runs a nursery on the edge of the Welsh mountains, specializing in unusual house plants, especially gesneriads. Their main income comes from wholesale growing of streptocarpus, a plant which may yet exceed African violets in popularity.

Also originating from southern Africa, streptocarpus are actually easier to grow than African violets, and if anything have a wider colour range. Rex not only grows them but is also involved in breeding, currently introducing several new cultivars and hybrids onto the market every year. From deep and smoky purples to the most subtle of lavenders, potent red-pinks to pristine whites, and very often with attractive throat markings, his streptocarpus deserve every bit of their increasing popularity. But so too do most other members of the family, and a poke around the Dibleys' glasshouses reveals scores of interesting and attractive gesneriads that just cry out for a place on a windowsill.

So, apart from the gesneriad family, what other flowering plants are there for softly lit conditions? Orchids for one, and they have a whole section of their own starting on page 107. The so-called forest cacti are another, cacti that are quite unrecognizably related to the familiar sun-loving spiny desert dwellers. The forest cacti grow as epiphytes, clinging to the branches of trees in mountain forests in South America, along with orchids and bromeliads. Their leafy stems are peculiar rather than beautiful but all is forgiven when they flower, the Christmas cactus (*Schlumbergera bridgesii*, *Zygocactus truncatus*) in midwinter, the Easter cactus (*Rhipsalidopsis gaertneri*, *Zygocactus gaertneri*) in early spring, and most of the others (*Rhipsalidopsis* and *Epiphyllum*) a little later still. Brightly coloured flowers in a variety of pink and apricot shades are very much the feature of those commonly cultivated, and the number of new cultivars of the

PLANTS AND PORCELAIN

African violets and other gesneriads do very well in sunless but light conditions such as those found in the corner of this room. The miniatures in particular have a jewel-like quality which goes well with porcelain and delicate objets d'art. (p.143)

smaller *Zygocactus* species is increasing all the time. The large-flowered orchid cacti, *Epiphyllum*, are now not as popular as once they were, perhaps because they resemble nothing more than bits of scruffy seaweed when not in bloom, but don't be put off as their flowers are spectacular. All these forest cacti come from climates with a distinct cool and dry season, and are notorious for not flowering again unless they are given a good rest, which means being put outside in a lightly shaded place for the summer and not watered too often or fed.

Begonias are one of the most useful, popular and varied groups of indoor plants, some loved for their bright and cheerful flowers, others for the magnificence or intricate patterning of their leaves. The flowering kinds are popular as bedding plants or short-lived pot plants, few other flowers producing such concentrated colour, ideal for brightening light but sunless windowsills. There are some flowering begonias which can be kept from year to year, chiefly the large-flowered tuberous-rooted kinds, the plants being dried off in the autumn to overwinter as dry tubers. However, the majority are not easy or particularly rewarding to keep for more than one season. Better to take some cuttings late in summer, which are very easy to root, and so start with vigorous new plants the following year.

The foliage begonias are evergreen and much longer lived than the flowering kinds, although they do need careful attention; particular

ALMOST A TREE

Aralias, like Polyscias scutellaria, *are grown as much for their branching stems as for their leaves, which give them a distinguished, almost tree-like appearance. (p.143)*

problems are fungal rots and moulds caused by overwatering or cool damp conditions, and leaf scorch caused by too much direct summer sun. Given the right place and care, they can quickly develop into magnificent plants. The large-leaved *Begonia rex* group add a touch of Victorian elegance to a room, and make wonderful centre-pieces for tables as the plants will form symmetri-

cal mounds of foliage if they are turned regularly so that all parts of the plant have a spell in the light. Their richly coloured and patterned leaves are among the most beautiful in the plant world, some silvery, others banded or veined in shades of green, grey, brown and purple. Wavy or hairy edges or crinkly surfaces are an additional feature of many of these begonias.

The smaller 'eyelash begonias', cultivars or hybrids of *Begonia bowerae*, are more suitable for vacant corners or narrow shelves. They have most beautifully patterned green and brown leaves with long hairs at the edges, hence the common name. Plants that are three or more years old start to trail, producing a cascade of dappled leaves.

Lastly there are those evergreen begonias that have attractive leaves and colourful flowers, many of them growing quite tall, such as the well-known trout begonia, *B. argenteo-guttata*, or the fuchsia begonia, *B. fuchsoides*. A particular feature of many of these is the combination of green leaves and soft red-pink flowers. Old and tall plants are quite stunning but tend to be top heavy and rather brittle, so needing careful positioning to avoid potential disasters.

One final flowering plant deserves mentioning – the impatiens, known as busy lizzies for their long season of flowering. Familiar as summer bedding or patio plants, they are able to continue flowering in somewhat lower light conditions than most of the plants used for these purposes, which makes them more appropriate for the home. They will even flower through the winter, but only if they can get an hour or two of direct sun occasionally. Modern hybrids mean that not only can you select plants for their colourful flowers but also for foliage, the dark leaves of many being the perfect complement to red, pink or white flowers.

After flowers, variegated foliage is many people's choice. Not only is it often colourful over a longer period, but it has the ability to brighten the area where it is placed. The situation itself needs to be light enough for the plant, but given this, the plant can be used to provide a contrast with dark furnishings or gloomy background.

Some of the best widely available plants for this purpose are the variegated weeping figs, especially *Ficus benjamina* 'Starlight', whose leaves are very pale cream with green splashes.

For a hot look, crotons, *Codiaeum*, are hard to improve on. With leaves that vary in shape from the very narrow to the very broad, and patterned with a mixture of red, orange, yellow and brown, crotons can seem like a ray of equatorial sun beaming into the room. However, they do need constant warmth (not below 15C/60F), reasonable humidity, good light, including some direct sun in winter, and a watering regime that never lets them dry out. If these conditions seem too demanding, the even more colourful coleus are a more easy-going alternative for cooler spots and, being faster growing, they will recover much more quickly from periods of neglect. They do need better light though, including plenty of direct sun. Occasionally called the 'poor man's croton' coleus probably display a more bewildering variety of leaf colouring and patterning than any other plant.

Dracaenas and cordylines, with their palm-like trunks that sprout tufts of narrow leaves at the top, are familiar office plants, their ease of cultivation and dynamic spiky profile making them appropriate to business environments. Maybe they are not restful enough for every home, but their tall habit makes them a useful centrepiece for plant groups and they usually make splendid specimen plants. Most of those sold are variegated, with either white-striped leaves, such as *Dracaena deremensis* 'Warneckii' or marked with red and yellow like the more cold tolerant *D. marginata* 'Tricolor'.

More widely grown are the ornamental figs, *Ficus* species. The ubiquitous rubber plant, *F. elastica*, has been around for such a long time it can look dated, epitomizing the 1960s, but given time it will grow big and majestic enough to outgrow any such worries. Even more common today is the weeping fig, *F. benjamina*, a plant whose great virtue is that even when quite young it has a tree-like form, a result of its tightly branching habit. It is also extraordinarily graceful, a word that can hardly be used to describe the chunky rubber plant. These figs are very tolerant; they will survive in quite low light conditions for several years and, if introduced to it gradually, will also thrive in direct sun. They can cope with the occasional lapse in watering and are less bothered by dry air than many plants. Other less commonly available figs are not quite so tough,

Greening the City

Two standard gardenias, grown largely for the heavenly scent of their flowers, and several other plants, including a stately ming aralia and a winter-flowering orchid, bring elements of a tropical garden into a city apartment. (p.143)

but easy enough. Why not try *Ficus rubiginosa*, *F. aspera* or the very compact mistletoe fig, *F. deltoidea diversifolia*, named for its small berries?

The ivy and aralia family is noted for its large number of fine foliage plants, among them the tree-like scheffleras. They tend to be tall growing with leaves composed of several leaflets that radiate out from the top of the stalk. Some have become very popular for the same reason as the weeping fig – a tree-like appearance and ease of cultivation. The widely available *Schefflera arboricola* (*Heptapleurum arboricola*) and its various variegated forms will make a good tall plant in time, but can also be persuaded to stay bushy and branch out if the tip of the main stem is removed, ideally when no more than a metre (3ft 3in) tall.

Many plants of the ivy and aralia family have a tendency to produce different shaped leaves at different stages of maturity; something of a nightmare for botanists! The appropriately named *Schefflera digitata* (*Dizygotheca elegantissima*) is one of the most graceful of all foliage house plants for good indirect light, with its darkly coloured, narrow leaflets and upright habit. It does need some care, however; sudden changes in temperature, drops below 10C (50F), or drought cause it to lose its leaves distressingly fast. It will eventually grow tall, to around 1.5m (5ft) and then start to develop its less elegant but still beautiful mature foliage, very dark in colour, broader and with more toothed margins.

The aralias, *Polyscias*, are popular in North America for their miniature tree-like habit, upright stems bearing branches covered with very finely divided leaves in the case of the Ming aralia, *P. fruticosa*, or the deep green round leaves of *P. balfouriana*. Attractive as mini-trees they will eventually grow into quite large plants. They are reasonably easy provided that they do not have to put up with dry air conditions, so mist them frequently with water.

A well-grown aralia is a good example of a plant worth growing for the beauty of its form, rather than the colour of its foliage or flowers. Flowers and colour are what immediately attract, often blinding us to the more subtle charms of fine leaves or elegant branches. One of the most intriguing selections of plants I have ever come across was in a shop in New York, and there wasn't a flower in sight. The owner, Larry Nathanson, selects his range of plants on the basis of shape and form, so alongside obviously sculptural plants like cacti and succulents, there are aralias chosen for their stems or branching habit, dracaenas with bent or contorted stems, multi-headed ponytail palms, *Beaucarnea* species, and miniature trees with plaited trunks. Sculptural plants like these, or others bought on the basis of their leaves and stems, will have a much longer season of interest than the vast majority of flowering plants.

Of the smaller plants that flourish in subdued light conditions one of the most popular groups are the peperomias, which display a wonderful array of leaf shapes and colours. Their neat and nicely compact shapes give them a distinctively 'pet-like' quality, an effect which is accentuated by their rather odd 'rat-tail' flower spikes. *Peperomia caperata* is the best known, with its crinkly leaves. The *P. obtusifolia* Magnoliaefolia group have fleshy rounded leaves often splashed with silver, while *P. argyreia* has silver and green stripes. As may be guessed from their succulent feel, peperomias do not have constant moisture in the wild; they grow on the floor of forests in South America, in areas with a distinct dry season. Consequently they need watering with care, being allowed to dry out slightly between waterings and with little in winter. In addition they are quite tolerant of a dry atmosphere, and their size makes them ideal for narrow windowsills.

Once you have learnt to appreciate light from a plant's point of view you will be able to look around your home with new eyes, spotting those places where there is enough light for plants to grow successfully, but also those where it is simply too dark for them to survive long. In most homes there are many areas that see little of the sun but, nevertheless, are undeniably light. These are where the plants in this section belong, along with most of those climbers, trailers and bromeliads described on pages 89 to 105.

A COLLECTOR'S WINDOWSILL

*There are hundreds of different African
violets and serious enthusiasts will
cram them onto every available
windowsill. One of their advantages
is that they can flower for most of
the year given good light and
adequate warmth. (p.144)*

COTTAGE WINDOW COLOUR

Opposite. *Streptocarpus are colourful but never garish, making them ideal for quiet country colour schemes. Don't worry if the long leaves begin to turn yellow at the tips or give* *every appearance of dying back. This is quite natural and a feature of these plants, some of which only have one leaf. To tidy up the foliage, just cut it back to healthy green. (p.144)*

STREPTOCARPUS PALETTE

Above. *'Streps', as they are known to their admirers, are one of the most rewarding groups of flowering indoor plants, having a long season and being very easy — more so in fact than their more widely grown cousins the African violets. Many new* *hybrids are being produced every year. Those with large trumpet-shaped flowers, sometimes referred to as Cape primroses, were once the most popular, but the more graceful small-flowered varieties are rapidly gaining ground. (p.144)*

A LEAFY LOUNGE

Left. *Two striking foliage plants, a palm and, in the corner, a philodendron, add an extra dimension to this living room. The climbing philodendron is attached to a moss pole, which enables it to be free standing. (p.144)*

BEAUTIFUL BEGONIAS

Above. *We are used to bright, brash, bedding begonias, but there are many other, more subtle species and varieties with interesting combinations of flowers and attractively marked and shaped leaves. Such plants go well with the quiet and homely decor of this country house. (p.144)*

FOLIAGE FORMS

Opposite. *A selection of small foliage plants illustrates the wide range of different leaf shapes and colours that can be combined in a limited space. Many of these plants are, by nature, woodland floor dwellers and so do not need too much light. Here they receive a little of the morning sun in an otherwise dark room. The interesting round, or peltate, leaves belong to* Pilea peperomioides *a native of China. (p.145)*

IN SOLITARY SPLENDOUR

Above. *The eyelash begonias are some of the best of all house plants for good but soft light. Such conditions are satisfied by this windowsill which receives several hours of sunlight a day. Not only are the leaves of this handsome* Begonia bowerae *'Tiger' most attractively marked and edged with long 'eyelash' hairs, but the plant is compact and easy to grow and occasionally bears white flowers, as shown here. (p.145)*

WASHING UP
WITH FLOWERS

Right. *The plants featured here are all members of the versatile gesneriad family. The tall kohleria in the centre not only has red-tinted leaves which look dramatic when lit from behind, but also tubular red flowers, patterned with tiny spots. Like many gesneriads it can be propagated from rhizomes. (p.145)*

RUSSET TONES

Above. *Achimenes 'Glory', left, and Aeschynanthus 'Big Apple', on the right, blend in with the warm colours of this late summer flower arrangement. Achimenes are cheerful and reliable summer-flowering plants that come in a variety of colours, flowering for a few months before dying back to tiny tubers, resembling pine cones, for the winter. (p.145)*

FOUR IN ONE

Opposite. *This plant is actually four! Several seedlings of* Pachyma *have been plaited together to create what appears to be a single specimen. Careful pruning will be needed to maintain the symmetrical umbrella of foliage on, what amounts to, a very particular kind of bonsai. (p.145)*

THE LATEST PINK

Above. *Syngoniums have always been valued for the subtle colouring of their leaves, but this is a new cultivar in pink, very unusual as a leaf colour. The soft indirect light, plenty of warmth and steamy humidity of this bathroom make it the ideal environment for such a forest-floor plant. (p.145)*

GREENING THE GLOOM
Plants for shade

We may not think of our homes as shady places, but as far as plants are concerned they are. Few parts of the home receive direct sun for more than a few hours a day, and many places never see it. Much of the average home is, unfortunately, just too dark for many plants, especially those that flower. This is a fact we have to resign ourselves to, unless, that is, we are keen enough to install special lighting for plants. So, looking around at all those table tops, corners and shelves where a plant would look great but the situation is rather too dark, what are we to do?

First of all remember there are plants that thrive permanently in such conditions in the wild. They may not be the most colourful, but they will introduce a welcome touch of green. Other possibilities include using light-loving plants, but moving them around so that they are not condemned to spend their lives in gloom, and have, say, half the year in good light. And, in some circumstances, it is possible to grow light-loving plants permanently in the shade, so long as active growth is discouraged.

Cool dark areas, hallways or corridors that are never heated to the same extent as other parts of the house, are perhaps the easiest to cope with.

POST-MODERN ASPIDISTRAS

Aspidistras usually give an instantly Victorian or Edwardian ambience to a room. But not so here, as this stark and modern setting liberates them from all traces of their past. (p.145)

Ferns are the obvious denizens for such places as many grow naturally beneath dense tree cover. However, they are also used to damp air conditions, although in cooler areas of the home, dry air is unlikely to be a problem. The popular maidenhair fern, *Adiantum raddianum*, is ideal for cool shady situations, the light green fronds having a freshness that can do much to enliven a dull corner. However, try growing it in warmer rooms where the relative humidity is lower, and you will find that it turns brown and dry.

There are several other ferns available, including many that are more robust than the maidenhair. Some of the most intriguing and rewarding are *Davallia*, sometimes called squirrel or hare's foot ferns, from the hairy stems that grow out horizontally over the surface of the compost and eventually over the side of the pot. These ferns are quite fast growing and will tolerate dry air better than many. The most tolerant of all must be the familiar Boston fern, *Nephrolepis exaltata*, which actually needs more light than most ferns and is quite tolerant of dry air.

Like ferns, ivies, *Hedera*, were great Victorian favourites, and similarly they do well in cool shady places, although ivies have the advantage of being more tolerant of dry air and absent-minded watering. They are versatile plants and can be grown as climbers up trellis or poles, or allowed to trail down from a pot. There are innumerable cultivars, those with silver and gold variegation being especially valuable for bringing a touch of glitter to a shady spot. ×*Fatshedera* is a hybrid between the common ivy and a much larger and

A SHADY CORNER

The parlour palm, to the left, and Boston fern both tolerate low light levels and bring a welcome touch of green to many a dark corner of the home. The taller dracaena, on the right, is reaching up into the light coming from above. (p.145)

shrubby plant, *Fatsia japonica*. It looks rather like a giant ivy, but has a more self-supporting habit. Although it won't cope with the dark nooks and crannies that ivies take in their stride, it will cope with reasonably shady conditions.

Warm shady conditions tend to be much more of a problem than cool shade, and such places constitute large areas of the home. Those parts of the living room or bedroom furthest from the windows, or the area directly beneath a window, can be surprisingly dark. Few ferns will really thrive in these situations as the humidity is not really high enough; if it were, you could grow some utterly magnificent house plants, but you would feel uncomfortable and the carpets might rot! One fern that does well at average room temperature and humidity, however, is the bird's nest fern, *Asplenium nidus*, which has large pale green leaves that are entire, not divided like most ferns. It has a symmetrical, formal appearance and can look outstanding grouped with other plants, or on its own in solitary splendour, on a pedestal for instance.

One of the finest plants for poor light is the cardamon, *Elettaria cardamomum* (the spice is made from the seed pods). Its dark green leaves, which when crushed release a pungent smell, are very attractive, and the plant is able to grow in a very wide range of light conditions and be remarkably tolerant of neglect. It will actually grow quite quickly if given a little bit of care, regularly watered and fed, which makes it a more interesting plant to share one's life with than an aspidistra which hardly seems to grow at all.

The incredibly tough but rather dull aspidistra is one of several old Victorian favourites ideal for low light conditions. Together with the 'parlour palms' it has been tried and tested by generations of coal fires and gas lights. Although most palms are large light-loving plants, the parlour palms are among those that originate in the gloom of the rain forest floor and make excellent indoor plants. *Chamaedorea elegans* is the best known but there are many others that deserve to be more popular.

After a period of relative obscurity, palms are coming back into fashion. They have a potent ability to transform the appearance of a room. Their height makes an immediate impression, but the relatively narrow shapes of the shade-tolerant species do not take up too much space. One of their most enthusiastic proponents is Martin Gibbons, who runs London's Palm Centre. Once an interior designer, his love of palms overran the house and he now works with them full time.

Looking very much like an intrepid nine-teenth-century explorer, it is not surprising to learn that Martin undertakes collecting trips to tropical and sub-tropical parts of the world in search of species that might be suitable for cultivation. Although his main interest is in the hardier palms, his shop has a good selection of those that flourish as house plants. Various species of *Chamaedorea* (*C. seifrizii* and *C. costaricana*) are very attractive with their bamboo-like stems. Or the various species of *Rhapis*, which have dark green hand-shaped leaves and a distinctively stylish aura, equally at home in period or modern interiors. Of all the palms, perhaps the toughest is *Howea forsteriana* which seems to be able to survive an incredible amount of neglect. Its large arching leaves, divided into broad dark leaflets, are so associated with the late Victorian era, that the mere placing of this plant in a room can conjure up a powerful sense of turn-of-the-century elegance.

The dark and dank floor of the tropical rain forest has been the source of many of the most highly valued indoor plants, many with large broad leaves decorated variously with coloured stripes and splashes. They will flourish in warm rooms provided that a certain level of humidity can be maintained. 'A touch of the tropics' beginning on page 81 looks at the larger of these plants in more detail. The smaller forest floor plants will fit into more conventionally domestic surroundings, though. The various marantas, whose leaves look almost as if they have been created by a textile designer, are particularly good as house plants, accepting lower temperatures and lower levels of humidity than many tropical plants. Their squat, compact shape renders them suitable for smaller, intimate spaces. *Maranta leuconeura* var. *kerchoveana* is the most familiar, but the slightly larger *M. leuconeura* var. *erythrophylla* (*M. tricolor*) is absolutely stunning.

Pileas are another useful group of compact plants that are tolerant of low light. The leaves may be highly coloured or marked with silvery blotches, such as the aluminium plant, *Pilea cadierei*, or in the case of the moon valley plant, *P. mollis*, marked with a dense network of sunken veins. Fittonias, too, are compact, low-growing plants with colourful pink or white venation. The great advantage of these compact little plants is that they provide colour and interest in places where flowering plants will not usually thrive, and their size means that they will not overwhelm their surroundings.

All these forest floor plants welcome a reasonable level of humidity. This can be provided either by daily misting with water or by standing them on trays of gravel kept permanently damp (less work!); the water will evaporate providing a more humid microclimate around the leaves. Browning leaves are a sign that the air is too dry for them.

The rather limited range of plants that flourish in shady places can be extended considerably if plants are moved around the home. A foliage plant can be kept in a place that would normally be too dark for it for several months and then moved to a lighter position for at least some of the warmer part of the year to stimulate healthy growth. With a little organization and imagination a number of plants can be rotated in this fashion. The rhapis and howea palms mentioned above benefit from this procedure, as do philodendrons, spider plants, scheffleras, tradescantias and asparagus ferns. Even cacti and succulents can be treated in this way, living in a sunny window or outside in the summer, to be moved into a darker place during the winter, when they go dormant. Some plants benefit greatly from a summer holiday outside; spider plants, for example, which can look terribly anaemic if kept indoors all year will form sturdy, well-coloured growth if put out for the summer.

There are a number of provisos with this strategy of rotation. One is that when plants are moved from weak light to strong it is done gradually, with a few weeks to acclimatize in a half-way house. Once I badly scorched the young growth on a friend's schefflera by moving it from a very dark corner to a west-facing conservatory, and had to wait several months for a new set of leaves to grow that were accustomed to the much higher light levels. Another point which can't be stated too often is that plants that do need a lot of light during their growing season.

Some foliage plants can be grown quite successfully for a number of years at lower than optimum light levels if they are kept static – in other words they are not encouraged to grow. Philodendrons, yuccas, dracaenas and ornamental figs are examples. Feeding and watering are kept to a minimum, to keep the plants ticking over, as new growth would be pale and stretched. While this approach may suit some people, and can work well in office environments, it probably does not appeal to keen gardeners, who want to experience the drama and mystery of growth.

Keeping plants in shady areas of the home can be a challenge, but it is not impossible. You will have much greater chances of success in greening the gloom if you remember that most shade lovers are used to humid forest floor conditions and so it is essential to try to avoid dry air. A tray of wet gravel or a container of damp compost into which the plant pots are sunk can work wonders with ferns and other shade lovers. So, don't be afraid of the dark, fill it with foliage.

WHERE EAGLES DWELL

Opposite. *These plants flourish in the soft light at the back of a room, well away from the window. Eventually the palm will grow large and develop attractive bamboo-like stems, but only after many years and several repottings, while its companions remain small and compact. (p.145)*

SKYLIGHT HIGHLIGHT

Above. *Under a skylight can be an ideal situation for the right plant, but don't place it too far below because leaves and stems will become very stretched and weak. In this instance, the backlighting does wonders for a maidenhair fern. (p.145)*

A Wreath for the Emperor

Opposite. *The Roman Emperor Hadrian stares out from a bower of greenery formed by the versatile and vigorous grape ivy* and a fern, one of the *Pteris tribe, somewhat more tolerant of dry air than the maidenhairs.* (p.145)

Some Like it Damp

Above. *Bathrooms are often the ideal places to grow ferns, being cool, shady and humid. Moist air is vital for the selaginella, from the rain forest floor, to thrive. Forms of this moss-like plant are also available with variegated and yellow-green foliage. (p.146)*

BATHROOM JUNGLE

Left. *Shade- and humidity-
loving plants such as ferns, a
spathiphyllum, top left, and a
maranta, in the forefront, relish
sunless bathroom conditions.
Here the delicacy of the fern
foliage makes a pleasing contrast
with the bolder leaves of the
other plants.* (p. 146)

MATCHING THE PAINTWORK

Above. *The leafy theme created
by the plants in this bathroom is
continued on the walls. The
large phlebodium fern – now
classified as a* Polypodium *–
was popular in the nineteenth
century, but is now quite rare.
This is a shame as its arching
fronds and bluish toned leaves
are striking.* (p. 146)

A Touch of the Tropics
Keep up the heat

Imagine how different your home could be by adding a few really dramatic plants. They could set the tone of a room or even the whole house or flat. Some indoor plants are capable of transporting you, as if on a magic carpet, away from the drizzle, grey skies or urban landscape that sulks at you through the window, away to a faraway land of sun and spicy flavours. To conjure up such a tropical mood means choosing the right plants and having the courage to use them big or in massed displays.

This scheme does not have to involve plants that need high temperatures. Palms, for instance, however hardy will do much, psychologically, to warm their surroundings. *Chrysalidocarpus lutescens* and *Howea forsteriana* do not need high temperatures (10C/50F minimum), and *Phoenix* species are happy down to below freezing. *Fatsia japonica* is totally hardy, but its large and lush leaves will also help to create an illusion of tropical climes.

There are, however, many plants from warm climates that thrive in the home and can be used to create a more genuinely tropical environment. The vast majority of these are happy with a winter minimum of 15C (60F), or in most cases an absolute low of 13C (55F). These

plants are often from the tropical rain forests, growing naturally on the forest floor where light is poor and so admirably suited for shady conditions in the home. They will grow much more slowly at room temperature than they would in their natural environment, but given the size that some of them can reach this is no bad thing. A reasonable level of humidity is important, especially for keeping up the appearance of their leaves. Maintaining the required humidity is difficult at higher temperatures, as many heating systems create an atmosphere that is very dry, too dry for many plants and indeed for people too. This problem can be overcome by various simple techniques; for instance, stand plants on trays of wet gravel, or place humidifiers on radiators.

The glory of these rain-forest plants is nearly always in the foliage; it is lush and often beautifully patterned, with an extraordinary variety of colours and designs. The selection available in shops is only a tiny proportion of the number of species that exists in the wild. But, sadly, massive habitat destruction is constantly reducing the number of wild species. If the range of plants in commercial cultivation does increase it may well have something to do with Barry Finden, who has made his life's work out of cultivating tropical exotics. His collection, now open to the public as a miniature rain forest under glass and built up over the years by swapping plants with other collectors, is now of major importance. He has several species that are almost extinct in the wild, and the hopes are that they can be re-introduced by propagating from his stocks. He also hopes to

TROPICAL DECADENCE

Exotic plants with expansive leaves envelop this chaise longue *to create a sultry scene, waiting to be filled by characters from a novel set in an outpost of the Empire. (p.146)*

be able to interest commercial propagators of house plants to take on some of his more decorative species and cultivars.

Wandering through Barry's steamy glasshouses, I am struck primarily by the foliage of the arum family, some of which are familiar, but others excitingly new. Dieffenbachias, for example, have leaves splashed in different shades of green; anthuriums with large arrow- or heart-shaped leaves. *Anthurium* and *Spathiphyllum* include species which are quite common as house plants, such as the flamingo flower, *Anthurium scherzerianum*, with its almost plastic-looking red flowers, and *Spathiphyllum wallisii*, known as the peace lily, which has white arum-like flowers.

Some of the most striking foliage belongs to species of *Alocasia*, huge heart-shaped leaves with dramatic veining, or of a quilted appearance, or sometimes a sheen that is almost metallic. Very few of these are in common cultivation as house plants, and yet they are all worthy of a try. Those of us who have grown them indoors have found them remarkably easy, and we can only hope that they become steadily more available.

Along with the arum family, the other tropical forest plants that catch the eye are often members of the maranta family. *Maranta leuconeura* in its various colourful forms we have already met in the previous section on plants for shady places. Needing slightly higher temperatures (13C/55F minimum) the bigger calatheas offer some of the most intricate and colourful foliage designs around. Their oval leaves are a restful, almost friendly shape, and move constantly in response to changes in the direction of the light. Most elegant of all, in my opinion is *Ctenanthe oppenheimiana*, which has grey and green striped paddle-shaped leaves on very tall stems.

Members of the banana family have vast floppy leaves radiating out from a rough stem composed of old leaf bases. True bananas, members of the genera *Musa* and *Ensete*, make good house plants provided their need for reasonably good light, including some direct sun every day, is satisfied. They need plenty of space as some can get very big! But there are dwarf varieties, and some of these are quite tolerant of low temperatures, even down to freezing in the case of *Musa basjoo*. Of all indoor plants, bananas have perhaps the greatest ability to transport one's imagination to far-away and warm places.

A 'tropical island' in the home is easily created anywhere warm, away from more than a few hours of direct sunlight or sources of hot dry air. Grow the plants in lush groups and in this way they will help each other create a moist microclimate. Combine them with tropical climbers like philodendrons and a Swiss cheese plant, *Monstera deliciosa*, for an exotic grouping in a corner of a room, or my favourite place, around a comfortable armchair. Smaller tropicals like marantas or syngoniums can be grown on tables or shelves to continue the theme. Given their love of humidity, bathrooms are ideal for tropicals.

What about tropical flowers? Unfortunately most need higher light levels than most homes are able to provide, but there are some that will thrive. The climber stephanotis is one, with a fragrance that truly speaks of far-away and steamy climes. Begonias, hibiscus, bromeliads and orchids, of course, are also tropical or subtropical and will grow well with the foliage plants referred to above if there is enough light. Even if there isn't, they can join a group temporarily for the duration of their flowering. *Phalaenopsis* orchids, coming as they do from the rain forests of Southeast Asia and requiring soft light and humidity, are ideal permanent partners.

Given certain basic requirements, tropical plants are surprisingly easy to grow and immensely rewarding. They thrive in the same conditions as we do, but they have an ability to conjure up very different world from our own.

MUSIC WITH PLANTS

Tropical plants flourish in a room that receives only the minimum of direct sunlight. Anthurium crystallinum *in the foreground, rarely seen in garden centres, is an easy foliage plant. Equally unusual is the sight of mature foliage on the* Schefflera, *or* dizygotheca, *in the corner.* (p.146)

TROPICAL EVOCATION

Right. *These plants – palms,
daturas, a cycad and the succulent*
Pachypodium *– help to evoke a
hot tropical atmosphere, although
in fact they will flourish in quite
cool conditions. Extending the
theme to the terrace beyond
enhances the illusion of warmer
climes. (p.147)*

FOREST FLOOR FOLIAGE

Above. *The arum family has
given us some of the finest indoor
foliage plants, such as the*
Spathiphyllum, Alocasia *and*
Calathea *pictured here. In
nature these plants grow in the
dark and dank conditions of the
tropical rain forest. (p.147)*

MAGNIFICENT MEDINILLA

Left. *Surely few plants deserve the description of voluptuous better than* Medinilla magnifica. *It thrives in a humid bathroom, flowering every summer for several months.* (p.147)

A TROPICAL CONSERVATORY

Above. *This imaginative planting was designed to remind the owners of their sojourn in Singapore. Surrounded by tropical climbers and other rain-forest plants, epiphytes cascade from the branch to which they are attached.* (p.147)

GREEN CASCADES
Climbers and trailers

limbers and trailers offer the opportunity to add a vertical dimension to indoor plant design. A climber going straight up or a trailer going straight down takes up little floor space but can make a dramatic effect visually. Climbers are extremely flexible: they can be persuaded to go sideways across walls, horizontally along ceilings, around banister supports, and perhaps most dramatically of all, across an invisible thread strung through the air.

There are relatively few climbing plants cultivated indoors. The reason is probably that most climbers, and certainly the vast majority of tropical ones, are by nature large plants. They climb in order to reach light above the forest canopy, using the stems of trees and shrubs for support, instead of growing on rigid stems of their own. It stands to reason that the majority of them are not only light lovers, but also have a strong desire to grow as fast as possible, and hence are unsuitable for the home. Nevertheless there are a number of lush and dramatic plants that can make excellent house plants.

Trailers are generally plants that are low growing in nature, scrambling over the ground or over rocks or sometimes growing epiphytically

A GALLERY FESTOONED

Every space in this small city house has been utilized to grow plants. The philodendron- and begonia-embroidered gallery is extremely unusual, allowing plants to feature dramatically but taking up little space. (p.147)

on the branches of trees in forests. Many climbers can be grown successfully as trailers: deprived of a support they will tumble down attractively.

The most common indoor climbers are tropical members of the arum family – philodendrons, scindapsus and the Swiss cheese plant, *Monstera deliciosa*. Fast growing in their native rain forests, they grow more slowly in the cooler environment of our homes, and thrive in well lit but sunless positions. They are often sold attached to poles filled with moss or a similar absorbent material, into which they plunge aerial roots that emerge from the side of the stem. Attached to such a pole they may live happily for years, especially if they are not encouraged to grow too much, by generous feeding or high temperatures. To be honest though, this is rather an unimaginative use of a climbing plant. Why not extend the moss pole by attaching one on top of another (they are fairly easy to obtain in garden centres) to encourage the plant to reach greater heights, or train it over trellis on a wall?

The sweetheart plant, *Philodendron scandens*, may be commonplace but it is certainly tough and well able to withstand neglect, and it is one of the most shade-tolerant species. With a bit of imagination it can be made a lot more interesting. It looks particularly good as a trailer, or used as a climber alongside other plants with contrasting foliage like the variegated weeping fig, *Ficus benjamina* 'Variegata', variegated peperomias or brightly coloured bromeliads. *Scindapsus aureus*, an attractively golden variegated relative of the sweetheart plant, is also hard wearing and copes well with shade, although the variegation might fade. It too is so familiar that its value can be overlooked, but put it with contrasting foliage and it is shown in a new light. Combine it with dark purple-leaved *Begonia rex* cultivars, for instance, or alongside dark-leaved *Philodendron erubescens* 'Burgundy' or 'Red Emerald'.

. There are quite a range of other philodendrons to choose from, mostly with big exotic-looking leaves. If encouraged to grow large these plants can create a powerful and magnificent display. The new leaves will turn to face the light, so the plant will look best trained over trellis or other vertical surfaces where the light is perpendicular to it. The best settings I have seen are on stairs where there is light coming from above, encouraging the leaves to spread horizontally.

What is true of the larger leaved philodendrons is even more so of the Swiss cheese plant, *Monstera deliciosa*. Yet how often do you see a really well-grown established plant outside a botanical garden? All too often the plants are not given enough light so that the leaves do not develop to their full size. Yet with care, a Swiss cheese plant can be among the most majestic of house plants. The secret is partly patience, leaving the plant in the same place for many years; partly good but soft light so the leaves can develop to the right size and degree of 'hole-iness'; and partly looking after the aerial roots. In nature these would cling to a tree trunk or branch and absorb moisture and nutrients, eventually taking over from the roots in the ground. Encouraging the aerial roots into a well-supported and sturdy moss pole, and then watering and feeding the pole by regular spraying will help a great deal. Or, less pleasing, but effective, copy the technique adopted by my local Indian take-away restaurant and direct the roots into bottles filled with water. Some care and a few years, and you can be well on your way to having a magnificent plant.

The most hard-wearing of all indoor climbers are the vines *Cissus antarctica* and *C. rhombifolia*. Not only will they take low temperatures in their stride, down to 7C (45F), but they are fairly tolerant of low light levels, especially *C. rhombi-*

CHAMPION SWISS CHEESE

The splendid size of these Swiss cheese plant leaves is partly due to them always having had plenty of light. Large climbers are best left undisturbed for years at a time, so their situation needs good forward planning. (p.148)

folia. As they have tendrils they can be easily trained onto trellis, wire or thread, and if watered and fed well will make rapid growth. They are thus ideal for quick and imaginative displays, although less exotic in appearance than the climbers of the arum family discussed above. To form a screen from floor to ceiling, place several vines in a row and train them up wires. Use invisible thread and they will grow through the air without visible means of support. They are also very effective as trailers.

Cool areas in the home, including quite shady places, are ideal for ivy, *Hedera*. The smaller-leaved English ivy, *Hedera helix* subsp. *helix* and cultivars, is able to climb by means of tiny aerial roots that cling to walls or other supports. The Victorians even encouraged ivy to climb the wall of the parlour, and there is no reason why you shouldn't do the same, so long as there is no need to redecorate for a good many years. There are innumerable ivies to choose from, with an enormous selection of different leaf shapes and levels of gold and silver variegation. Ivies' tolerance of low temperatures makes them ideal for places like porches and halls which may not be heated to the same level as elsewhere in the building, and those with silver leaves are particularly welcome to light up dark nooks and crannies.

Ficus pumila is related to the rubber tree and the other familiar tree-like figs, but is completely different in form, being a creeper which will cling to surfaces in the manner of ivy. It relishes shady humid conditions and can grow quite quickly, either as a trailer to cover the compost around larger plants or as a self-clinging climber for the adventurous indoor gardener.

There are few flowering climbers suitable for the home: most pine for the more generous light of the conservatory (see page 119). Stephanotis with its intensely, sometimes overpoweringly, fragrant flowers is one of the more practicable, so long as it can be given good subdued light, average warmth (winter minimum of 13C/55F) and fed well. As a twiner it needs the support of a wire or trellis. Also twining in habit are the hoyas, which flourish in similar conditions. Personally I love them, but they are not everyone's favourite: the mysterious bunches of little waxy star-shaped flowers, in shades of cream or maroon according to species, may be not colourful enough for all tastes.

Trailing plants are very versatile: they can be used to hang down bare stretches of wall, supported on wall-stands or from hanging brackets. The tops of cupboards and shelves are other obvious places, along with mantelpieces above unused fireplaces. Hanging baskets or suspended ornamental pot holders are another means of display, provided that they are in a position where no-one is at risk of colliding with them and that their supports can take the sometimes considerable weight of plant and wet compost. But perhaps the most elegant way of all to display a trailer is to have it tumbling down from an elegant pedestal.

The best known trailers are the tradescantias and their relatives, along with one of the most common house plants, the spider plant, *Chlorophytum comosum*, stalwart of church fêtes and charity sales up and down the land. These are remarkably tolerant plants, particularly of low temperatures, just above freezing being sufficient. Although they will survive neglect, who wants a plant that just survives? Like all living things they will look so much more attractive with care and attention. Above all they will

FERNS ON THE WALL

Three of these plants are ferns whose natural habit of growth makes them suitable for growing on pieces of bark which can then be hung on a wall. (p.148)

flourish in good light, the leaves will be better coloured and the growth sturdier. Indeed, spider plants often look best if they are stood outside during the summer. Temptingly easy to propagate to keep the charity plant stands going, these plants will all develop much better without having bits constantly snipped off. A mature spider plant with masses of 'babies' cascading down will look magnificent.

The asparagus ferns, not really ferns at all but true flowering plants, are also very familiar, and deservedly so as they are easy-going and particularly useful for shady places. Less common are the plectranthus group, also good indoor trailers. They belong to the mint family, and some have attractive leaves which smell of incense, such as the silver-variegated *Plectranthus coleoides* 'Marginatus'.

Flowering trailers are few. A situation with very good light, direct sunlight for much of the day, is suitable for trailing pelargoniums, which are certainly colourful, but always leggier in the house than when grown outside or displayed in a conservatory.

Columneas are undoubtedly the finest flowering trailers for the home. Members of the versatile gesneriad family, they plunge straight down over the side of the pot with stems covered in masses of small, generally dark leaves, tubular red, orange or yellow flowers flickering out sideways like tongues of flame. Related but stiffer in habit are the *Aeschynanthus*, with similarly coloured flowers. Recent hybridizing will, I hope, mean a wider range of these dramatic plants in the shops.

Perhaps more than any other group of plants, climbers and trailers require imagination, and even daring, in their use. They also demand long-term planning; when you buy a climber you need to think about what you are going to do when it reaches the limits of its support. Large climbers and their supports are unwieldy and will need to stay in the same place for many years. But with some consideration and a little artistic flair these plants can lend more than a touch of leafiness to the home.

SELF-CLINGING CREEPER

Opposite. *The creeping fig clings, ivy-style, to surfaces by means of the tiny adventitious roots along its stem. If you don't* *intend to redecorate for a number of years, then why not let one climb directly up the wall?* *(p.148)*

FILLING A CORNER

Above. *There is just enough light in this corner for some African violets and a versatile scindapsus to thrive. Some stems* *of the latter trail naturally, while others are trained along the wall by means of pins.* *(p.148)*

A WATERFALL OF LEAVES

Opposite. *This magnificent columnea sits on a mantelpiece over a disused fireplace. The weight of foliage is considerable and so a heavy clay or ceramic pot is necessary to keep the arrangement stable. When displaying such large plants make sure the shelf or support will bear the weight. (p.148)*

FIERY FLOWERS

Above. *A smaller columnea resides in a carved wooded holder mounted on a wall. The columneas are noted for their fiery tubular flowers produced late in the season and which, in the wild, are pollinated by humming birds. Many are native to Central America, and American growers, in particular, are raising lots of new and exciting cultivars. (p.148)*

Miniature Climber

Opposite. *The goose-foot plant in the corner climbs up a short length of moss pole by means of roots emerging from its stems. It* *is beneficial to keep the moss moist by spraying. The pole will serve for several years before an extension is needed. (p.148)*

Stairway Bower

Above. *From South America and the West Indies comes grape ivy, or* Cissus rhombifolia, *one of the most adaptable and shade-* *tolerant climbers for the house. Here it has been trained along the wall by means of pins and invisible thread. (p.148)*

LIVING ON AIR
Bromeliads – the born survivors

The bromeliad family has provided us with some of the most intriguing and beautiful indoor plants. Like most tropical orchids, bromeliads are primarily dwellers of the treetops, growing on branches high above the ground where there is far more light than in the gloom of the forest floor. Unlike orchids which are widely distributed throughout the tropics, bromeliads are almost exclusively American, being found in a variety of habitats from the deep south of the USA to latitude 50° south of the Equator.

Bromeliads are of value because they often have extremely ornamental foliage as well as flowers; their relatively compact and symmetrical form lends itself to interior decor and they are easy to look after. The so-called air plants, which can grow without roots, offer the most exciting possibilities to the imaginative and creative indoor gardener.

Bromeliads are born survivors, with an array of characteristics that enable them to cope with a variety of demanding environments, from rain forest to desert. The most bizarre are the puyas, which must deserve the title of the most sadistic plants in existence. Living in the harsh climate of the Andes, where soils are often extremely poor,

they supplement their nutrient supply by trapping birds inside a cage of inward pointing spikes on the leaves, leaving them to die and consequently to fertilize the soil at the base of the plant.

The majority of bromeliads are epiphytes, living on tree branches, in tropical or subtropical environments. Some live in rain forest proper, where there is a constant supply of water, others in more seasonal climates where they must survive several months every year without appreciable rain. One of the characteristics that most epiphytic bromeliads share is the central 'urn', formed by the bases of the leaves at the centre of the leaf rosette. This urn is used to catch and store water, to supplement or replace that which can be absorbed by the roots, whose main function in many species is that of anchorage to the tree branch or other surface on which the plant grows. Needless to say, watering is a simple task, a case of keeping the urn topped up during the growing season. In many tropical environments these miniature ponds are an oasis for wildlife, providing homes for insect larvae and the tadpoles of tree frogs. Indeed some species of insects and amphibians are totally dependent on bromeliad urns for their survival.

Only a tiny proportion of bromeliads are in cultivation, but some of these are very familiar house plants indeed – *Aechmea fasciata*, *Vriesea splendens* and *Neoregelia carolinae* forma *tricolor* being the most common. They are reliable, flourishing at average room temperatures, but needing reasonably high humidity. They do best in good light away from direct sun, but will

DRIFTWOOD HOME

A gnarled piece of driftwood is the perfect home for some air plants, as they can simply be pushed into holes in the wood, or else held in place with plastic-coated wire. (p.149)

BROMELIAD DIVERSITY

This bromeliad collection in a high-rise apartment is kept either in pots on a glass sheet on a table top, or suspended from the trellis above. Bromeliads have very small root systems, so do not need large pots, which makes hanging them up that much easier. (p.149)

certainly survive and stay attractive in poorer light. Watering is best done with soft water or rain water, and the urn should be emptied and refilled every few months: apart from anything else it can get stagnant and smelly.

Bromeliad 'flowers' are, on the whole, brightly coloured, the stems and bracts (a type of leaf that surrounds the flower buds) usually providing more colour and lasting much longer than the true flowers themselves. After flowering the rosette usually dies off, leaving one or more daughter rosettes to take over. Separating these young plants and removing the remains of the deceased parent are the only time that one ever need repot a bromeliad.

Of all the bromeliads the most extraordinary are the air plants, members of the genus *Tilland-sia*, which can literally live off the air. Their minimal root systems serve only to hold them onto a branch, water being absorbed directly from the atmosphere through special silvery hairs on the leaves, rather than being caught in a central urn. Nutrients are absorbed from minute dust particles that get caught in the hairs. The ultimate air plant must surely be Spanish moss, *Tillandsia usneoides*, so characteristic of much of the Americas from the southern USA down into tropical South America. Aptly named it forms long trailing grey growths that cling to tree branches, rocks, telegraph wires or whatever else that happens to trap one of the minute seeds.

Air plants come in a bewildering variety of shapes and sizes, often assuming 'animal-like' forms, recalling the inhabitants of a seaside rock pool such as sea-anemones, sea-urchins or star-fish. Some are very densely hairy, others smooth, some have rosettes of tightly packed leaves, others have relatively few. The leaves of some are straight, while others have leaves that are twisted and contorted.

The ability of air plants to live without roots means that they can be grown in a completely different way to most plants, scattered among ornaments, wedged or tied onto pieces of driftwood, made into mobiles, attached to branches to make a 'bromeliad tree' or incorporated into flower arrangements. Children are particularly attracted to them.

Air plants have become increasingly popular in recent years, as firms have tried to exploit their obvious appeal to the imagination of the public. However, they are often sold without proper instructions for their care, or glued to ornaments, which can fatally damage them, and thus many buyers have had disappointing results. Yet air plants are easy to look after if their basic needs are carefully met.

Mike Harridge and his wife, Liz, grow and sell air plants by mail order. They make sure that all their customers have a clear understanding of how to look after their purchases. The plants are all grown in a glasshouse on their premises in Leeds. Tillandsias from seed take four years to reach a saleable size and are grown from Mike's own seed stock.

He has always been very much against the collection of wild bromeliads, which has done much to reduce the numbers of some species in their native countries. Fortunately collection of bromeliads in the wild is now restricted by law in many countries and against the Convention on International Trade in Endangered Species of Wild Fauna and Flora (CITES).

Mike started growing bromeliads when he was twelve, in his native Sri Lanka, brought to them by an interest in the tree frogs that lay their eggs in the 'urns'. He first came to Britain when he was involved in importing water plants, moving on to work as a snake handler engaged in extracting venom for medical research. In 1977 he started selling air plants and other bromeliads in Britain, and is now a leading supplier.

Air plants are tolerant of a wide range of temperatures, down to 5C (40F), although they should be kept dry if temperatures get this low. Above 10C (50F) they will need regular water-ing, a mist spray being ideal for this purpose, and will need more frequent applications at higher temperatures. Mike explains that it is vital that air plants are allowed to dry out between water-ings, and are never allowed to sit in water, which will cause rapid decay.

As many air plants come from seasonal cli-mates, they can store water. This means they will survive for up to a month without moisture. They are very sensitive to chemicals, and should be watered with soft water, and kept well away from aerosol-delivered products, such as air fres-heners, hair sprays and cleaning materials. They

EXOTIC COLOUR SPLASH

Aechmea chiantinii *hails from the treetops of the Amazon basin. Its bright flowers provide a splash of colour among the darker foliage of other tropical plants, like the philodendron in the background.* (p.149)

should be fed with a liquid feed about six times a year, when they are in active growth.

Good light, but not direct sunlight is important to enable them to maintain their characteristic shape and colour. As good ventilation is essential, air plants are unsuitable for terrariums and other enclosed environments. If they are incorporated into flower arrangements or attached to ornaments they should never be glued, but gently wired or tied in position.

An interesting footnote to their botanical name, *Tillandsia*, dates back to the late eighteenth century when the plants were first brought to the attention of Carl Linnaeus, the Swedish botanist. It was noticed that species were highly sensitive to constant damp, which caused rapid decay. Linnaeus named them after Elias Tillands, another Swedish botanist, who had been famed for his terror of water, and who would travel hundreds of extra miles in order to avoid crossing over a bridge.

It is not just tillandsias that can be grown on 'bromeliad trees', but any of the epiphytic bromeliads including the smaller aechmeas, neoregelias and nidulariums. They will need to be securely tied on with nylon thread or plastic-coated wire, and some moss or green plastic netting tied around the base of each plant to encourage some rooting and hence better anchorage. In more humid conditions, a conservatory for instance, other epiphytes, notably orchids, can also be grown on tree branches.

Some bromeliads are terrestrial and need to grow in pots of compost in a more conventional manner. Among them are the billbergias and also the pineapple which makes a dramatic, if rather large and spiky house plant that can be cheaply grown from the top of a shop-bought fruit. More cheerful-looking and less likely to impale you is a variegated relative, *Ananas bracteatus* 'Tricolor' (*A. bracteatus* 'Striatus'), with gold-edged leaves.

Bromeliads, and air plants in particular, are one of the most fascinating and addictive groups of plants. They open up a whole range of possibilities for the artistic and imaginative indoor gardener.

PAINTED JUNGLE

Opposite. *A jungle fantasy comes to life with two flowering bromeliads:* Aechmea comata, *to the left, and* Vriesea splendens *in front of it. Like most bromeliads, the flower spikes will last for many months, bringing a truly exotic touch to wherever they are placed. (p.149)*

BILLBERGIA CASCADE

Above. *This cast-iron gallery is the perfect place to display the showy pink bracts and flower heads of a billbergia. It can then be admired from both above and below. (p.149)*

AIR BORNE

Opposite. *The most dramatic way to grow air plants! And growing them as a mobile ensures that these plants from the tree-tops of South America get all the ventilation they need. (p.150)*

BROMELIAD TREE

Above. *Well-shaped branches make an attractive and very naturalistic way of growing bromeliads, especially the smaller air plants. The pink plants, appropriately called earth stars, on the chest top are bromeliads too. (p.150)*

PERFECTLY SENSUAL
The intriguing orchids

rchid. The very name conjures up exoticism and luxury; the flower of the tropics, the heavy humid atmosphere of distant lands, the buttonholes and bouquets of the wealthy. In the popular imagination they are invariably expensive and difficult to grow, quite beyond the reaches of most ordinary gardening mortals who must remain content with seeing them only in high-class florists' windows, botanical gardens and the occasional fleeting possession of a spray – the memento of a special occasion, a family wedding perhaps, or the attentions of an ardent lover.

The appeal of orchids is complex and varied: some are undoubtedly extremely colourful or have potent scents, while others are quite undistinguished in colour – green, cream and brown – but charm through their shape or intricate markings. The flowers of many orchids have a powerful aura of sexuality, which must contribute much to their sub-conscious appeal. (In fact many have evolved their flowers to 'invite' insects to mate with them in order for pollination to take place.)

Early in their history orchids acquired a reputation as elite flowers, and once something becomes a status symbol, it acquires a rarefied

ELEGANT INTRICACY

While not all orchids are colourful, many deserve close attention for the intricacy of their markings and the unusual and graceful shape of their flowers. This Encyclia *is one of the cockle-shell orchids. (p.150)*

reputation that is not easily relinquished. Orchids are still very much on a pedestal even though, worldwide, many people of modest means grow them, and gain much pleasure and satisfaction from so doing. But they are still seen as somehow different to other plants, so it is not surprising that there is a major psychological barrier to growing them as house plants.

Orchids are not really that different; if you can grow other tropical and warm climate plants successfully in the home then you can grow orchids too. But as with all indoor plants it is crucial that the right species are chosen, and that their cultural needs are understood and responded to. There are some, the cymbidiums for example, familiar as wedding buttonholes, that are easy as glasshouse plants but very difficult to flower in the home because of their need for cool winter temperatures and high levels of light. Fortunately there are others, notably the 'moth orchids', *Phalaenopsis*, which are arguably easier to grow indoors than under glass. I would make one final general point: that while it does take skill to grow orchids really well, they are very difficult to kill – which is more than can be said for a great number of house plants!

The majority of cultivated orchid species are epiphytes, living in their native lands not at ground level but in the treetops, clinging to branches or trunks of trees in humid forests. There is more light high in the canopy, and no shortage of nutrients in the form of dead leaves and other debris. In seasonal climates, drought can be problem, so many have developed thickened water-storing stems, called pseudobulbs, to see them through times of scarcity.

Although orchids are numerous throughout the humid tropics, most of those grown today, or their wild ancestors, are from more limited areas. The mountain forests of South and Central America are home to many popular species of *Cattleya*, *Miltonia*, *Miltoniopsis* and *Odontoglossum*, for instance. The foothills of the Himalayas, around Assam, are another area that has provided many species in cultivation, notably *Cymbidium* and *Vanda*. Towards the Equator, the rain forests of Southeast Asia have given us *Dendrobium* and *Phalaenopsis*. African orchids have attracted relatively little attention, as they tend to be less colourful than their Asian and South American counterparts.

Orchids are almost invariably produced by specialist nurseries. Many have come and gone over the years, but one that has survived is Burnham Nurseries, in Devon, England. A real family business, it is now run by brother and sister team, Brian and Wilma Rittershausen, having been set up by their father in the 1940s. While many of the old firms that date back to earlier in the century specialized too much in one particular group of orchids and have consequently been unable to adapt to changing fashions, Burnham Nurseries have survived and expanded through growing a diversity of species and hybrids.

Brian Rittershausen has seen fashions come and go in orchid growing, as in other spheres of life. Once upon a time the best sellers were the big cymbidiums and showy cattleyas, grown in massed ranks under the glass of wealthy collectors. As the cost of heating glasshouses and paying staff has rocketed, these orchids have lost popularity, to be overtaken by smaller species, in particular those more suitable as house plants like *Phalaenopsis*, *Miltonia* and *Miltoniopsis*. Methods of propagation have changed too: there was a time

COMPACT AND COLOURFUL

Miltonias, like the closely related pansy orchids, make reliable house plants, although unlike many orchids they do not last long as cut flowers. Their flowering in late summer and autumn, and small size, means that they make good indoor plants. (p.150)

when nurseries like Burnham would have imported large numbers of species orchids that were collected wild, gathered from their treetop homes in the tropics. Greater awareness of the damage that this does to native populations, and the growing rarity of many orchids, has all but stopped this practice. Now plants are more likely to be propagated by division or from seed, while some can be micropropagated in laboratories.

The comparative difficulty and slowness of propagating orchids, compared with many other popular plants, accounts for their relative high prices. Modern micropropagation techniques which enable more plants to be produced over a shorter period of time are beginning to lower the prices of some orchids. This should make them more attractive to novice growers and I hope, widen the appeal of this exceptional family.

Before we consider the possibilities of growing orchids as house plants, we need to look at the conditions in which they flourish. As plants that live high up in the branches of trees, it comes as no surprise to learn that they need a combination of humidity and good ventilation. These two factors do not always go together, especially in the home, but they are essential for happy healthy orchids. Light and water requirements vary according to the type of orchid, and are no more demanding or tricky to provide than for many other house plants.

The main peculiarity of orchids as far as the indoor gardener is concerned is to do with compost. So different are orchid composts to other growing media, that many people simply cannot believe that a plant can grow in such material. Coarsely chopped pine bark, rockwool (the material used for roof insulation), polystyrene chunks, beads of plastic – all are used in different compost recipes. The factor they all have in common is that they provide exceptionally good drainage. These materials contain little or no nutrients, so feeding is important. Orchids, used to living the ascetic life in the treetops, have low nutrient needs compared to many indoor plants, and these can easily be met by using one of the proprietary orchid feeds now widely avail-

A SENSUAL TOUCH

The bathroom is a good place for many house plants and orchids are no exception. Here tropical shells make an appropriately exotic accompaniment to Phalaenopsis, *sometimes referred to as moth orchids. (p.150)*

able. It is very important to read and follow the instructions given on the packet, as orchids can be badly affected by too high levels of certain nutrients. Generally, little and often during the growing season is the rule, with an occasional dousing with lots of water, perhaps every few weeks, to flush out excess nutrients.

Knowing how much water to give is perhaps the greatest headache; I know it is for me. Given their intense dislike of wet and stagnant root conditions, it is much better to risk under rather than over watering. This may mean plants that don't do their best, but at least they will live for you to get it right in future; for a soggy orchid is a dead orchid. Species with pseudobulbs – thickened stems which store water – will need watering well when they are in active growth, with water being given when the compost starts to dry out. When they are dormant, they will need very little moisture. Orchids that come from climates where there is constant moisture tend not to have pseudobulbs, for example the *Phalaenopsis* from the constantly moist rain forests of Southeast Asia and the Philippines, as they do not need storage organs, and can grow and flower continuously.

So, given this basic outline of the needs of orchids, how practical are they as house plants? Any orchid can be brought into the home from the glasshouse and kept there while in flower, but how many are really suitable as year-round indoor plants? A plant that is going to live in the home permanently needs to look attractive at all times and, it has to be said, that with rare exceptions, orchids are not specially good looking out of flower. A windowsill of flowering cattleyas may look stunning, but when they are dormant it will be frightfully dull. We need to select either those that flower more or less non-stop, like *Phalaenopsis*, or those that are compact and unobtrusive when out of flower, such as *Miltoniopsis* or *Paphiopedilum* hybrids. Indoors it is better to have a few compact orchids that grow alongside other plants with different flowering times or attractive leaves, so that there is always something to greet the eye.

The best indoor orchids I have seen are in the home of Devon-based florist, Stuart Rodgers. There are orchids everywhere, especially his favourite white-flowered *Phalaenopsis*. As a guest, you wake up next to one on the bedside table, and then have breakfast surrounded by others, on the floor, on shelves, in corners, sometimes alone, sometimes with other exotics or with *objets d'art*. The predominant colours of the house are white, black and silver, and the white *Phalaenopsis* echo the walls, carpets and furnishings. Other brighter varieties provide occasional highlights of colour.

One of Stuart's secrets of success must be the quality of the light. The house receives little direct sunlight, which would scorch the leaves of rain-forest plants, and yet the house is filled with a diffuse light, reflected off the white walls. This allows orchids and the other plants, like anthuriums and caladiums, to flourish more or less anywhere. The temperature is ideal too. *Phalaenopsis* need a night-time minimum of 15C (60F), rising to 20C (68F) or more in the day, and although they will take lower temperatures this results in the flower buds dying. They will thrive at higher temperatures, 20–30C (68–86F), but the production of flowers is stimulated by the plants being kept somewhat cooler for part of the year. *Phalaenopsis* need humidity, and this can be provided by daily misting, and by standing pots on trays of moist pebbles. As plants from a continuously warm and damp climate they always need to be kept slightly moist.

SUBTLE STYLE

Many orchids display a subtle and particular beauty. Those, like the gongoras, which have flowers that hang downwards, need a certain ingenuity to show them at their very best. (p.150)

THE CLASSIC ORCHID

Cattleyas are what most people think of as the classic orchid – lush, colourful and flamboyant. This is, in fact, one of the robust hybrids between a Cattleya *and* Laelia. *While many have large and conventionally colourful flowers, there are others that are just as beautiful but much more unusual in colouring. (p.150)*

Paphiopedilums, known as slipper orchids from the distinctive shape of their flowers, also make good house plants. They flower for a more limited period than phalaenopsis, only during the winter and spring, and the flowers have quite a different appeal – a subtle and complex blend of browns, yellows, creams and greens. Their advantages are that they are compact, and their origins on the rain-forest floors of Asia means that they have a greater tolerance of lower light levels than most flowering indoor plants. You must take care to find out the temperature requirements at the time of purchase as these vary according to

variety – and there are an immense number of hybrids from which to choose. But all paphiopedilums will thrive at average room temperatures.

In contrast to the almost esoteric appeal of *Paphiopedilum* orchids, *Miltoniopsis* are almost childlike in their simplicity and gaiety. Not surprisingly called 'pansy orchids', their flat flowers come in a range of pinks and creams. Their small size makes them easy to accommodate and unobtrusive when not flowering, and they make excellent house plants. As epiphytes from quite high up in the tree canopy they need good, but diffuse light. They are happy in average room temperatures, with a winter minimum of 13C (55F).

Even if you have only one orchid, it is advisable to do some further reading about its cultural requirements (see page 156), as space permits me only to give a brief introduction to the extraordinary world of orchids. You will not only learn more about how to care for your plant, but your eyes will be opened further to the beauty and diversity of this captivating family.

AN ORIENTAL TOUCH

Opposite. *The last rays of the day's sun strike some pansy orchids,* Miltoniopsis *hybrids, and miltonias, grouped with the dark leaved* Begonia *'Cleopatra'. Like most orchids,* Miltonia *and* Miltoniopsis *thrive in good but indirect light. They hail from Central and tropical South America and possess pseudobulbs, a means of storing water. (p. 151)*

THE PHALAENOPSIS PAINTBOX

Above. *The moth orchids from tropical Asia are the most amenable orchids to centrally heated houses, and come in a variety of colours although white and pink are the most common.* Less common butter yellows and spotted hybrids have a special charm. To help them in their epiphytic lifestyle, they have masses of aerial roots and succulent leaves. (p. 151)

DINING WITH COMPANY

Left. *The orchids here would normally reside in a glasshouse or on a windowsill, but have been brought together to form a special decorative table feature. The silver and black theme of the surroundings is one that is appropriate to such a selection, as it allows the flower colours to be shown to best advantage.* (p.151)

HEAVENLY SCENT

Above. *Not outstandingly colourful, although with a distinct beauty of its own, Brassia verrucosa is an orchid with a wonderful scent, somehow quintessentially tropical and lingering but not overpowering. One or two of the long flower heads grow from the base of each pseudobulb of this tropical American orchid.* (p.151)

PURE AS DRIVEN SNOW

Opposite. *White* Phalaenopsis *are especially popular – indeed some people grow no other colour – and, of course, they fit in well with any colour scheme. The moth orchids can blossom almost* continuously, producing new flower spikes from along the stem of the older ones. They are compatible with human needs, sharing similar temperature requirements. (p.151)

FOREST FLOOR BEAUTY

Above. *Unlike most tropical species, the slipper orchids, or* Paphiopedilum, *are mostly terrestrial and grow under trees in tropical Asia. This means they are able to flourish in fairly low light conditions. Their* earthy colours may not charm everybody but the fact that they flower in winter gives them an extra appeal. There are many hybrids available and some species have mottled leaves. (p.151)

A WORLD APART
Making the most of conservatories

Conservatories are back in fashion. Whereas in their heyday during the Victorian era their main function was the ostentatious display of exotic plants, their revival now is more to do with creating an additional living room. Nevertheless, many conservatory owners are keen to create a living space in which plants feature strongly, and to make the most of the possibilities offered by year-round gardening.

The key to a successful conservatory is to get the right compromise between plant and human needs. In the house humans nearly always come first and plants have to fit in around them. In the conservatory, however, plant needs can be catered for to a greater extent. Some really keen indoor gardeners may want to use the conservatory simply as a glasshouse, as somewhere to grow the kind of plants that are not very successful as house plants, and to pack in as many weird and wonderful tropicals as they can. Most people, though, will want to use the conservatory as a garden room, an alternative green living room or dining room, and will not want to clamber through jungle-like vegetation to reach the table.

Flowers are the priority for many conservatory owners. There is so much more light than even the sunniest picture window lets in, and this makes it a far better environment for attractive flowering plants, like pelargoniums, plumbagos, bougainvilleas and passion flowers. With these kinds of plants it is possible to create somewhere quite different from either the house or the garden. Plants which are scented, either with fragrant flowers or aromatic foliage add another dimension, especially since the still air in a conservatory traps scent. Scented conservatory plants can effectively perfume the house, their fragrance wafting through connecting doors. Having a conservatory enables you to create an individual and very sensual world, one that is neither indoors nor outside, one that is always pleasant to sit in, whatever the weather outside.

Conservatories can be problematic though. If they face the sun for most of the day they can become insufferably hot, one's own little piece of the Nevada desert. Insect pests can be a problem, whitefly especially; quite apart from the damage that is being done to the plants, who wants to sit among hordes of tiny flies?

Careful thought needs to be given to the design of a conservatory, in particular to the direction it faces which will affect how much sun it receives, and when. Which is more important for your lifestyle, morning or evening sun? How much do you want to be able to sit in the sun in the winter? Good ventilation is vital, especially if it receives sun for much of the day, but you need good security between the house and the conservatory so you can leave windows open all day without worrying about intruders coming in with the cooling breeze. A sunny structure may well

BASKING UNDER GLASS

Sun-loving plants like oleanders and abutilons thrive in a light conservatory such as this one. Such situations offer an ideal place for us to enjoy the sun all year round too. (p.151)

need blinds as well, to keep both human and plant inhabitants cool and shaded.

An important feature often overlooked in conservatory construction is the border, an area in which plants can be grown directly in the soil (which will need to be dug over and enriched with organic material). This can make all the difference to some popular conservatory plants. Abutilons, bougainvilleas, cestrums, plumbagos and daturas, or *Brugmansia*, for instance, grow much better if their roots are allowed a free run rather than confined in pots. Besides which, these thirsty plants will not run short of water nearly so quickly when growing in open soil. If you want climbers to reach the roof for instance, then a well prepared soil border is an absolute must.

Plant size is another problem in conservatories: many of the popular plants from Mediterranean climates, including those mentioned above, are by nature large shrubs. Even when their growth is limited by being grown in pots, they can form substantial plants with surprising rapidity. So if you are growing them in the border then be prepared to hack your way back in with a machete after a holiday! In actual fact the vast majority of these shrubs will take very hard pruning, so there is no need to worry about being ruthless with the secateurs or saw. Some, like the almost non-stop flowering *Solanum rantonettii* and the larger cestrums, will benefit from a yearly cut back to ground level. In some cases climbers may be trained, unruly plumbagos for instance may be made into very attractive standards or trained to cover a wall.

Pests and diseases are frequently more of a problem in conservatories than either in the garden or the home, whitefly and red spider mite in particular. Chemical sprays are often ineffective, and anyway who wants to sit, let alone dine, in an environment regularly doused with potentially toxic chemicals? Fortunately, biological control is now available to deal with all major glasshouse pests, and if the instructions are carried out and the control introduced early enough in the season, it is usually very successful. Biological control basically means introducing

EXPLOITING THE SPACE

I have put up shelves in my own tiny inner city conservatory to maximize the amount of growing space. Such places are ideal for displaying trailers and small climbing plants. (p.152)

natural predators to go round and eat up the insect pests. Despite what you might think, the predators are almost totally unobtrusive as they go about their work.

The most popular conservatory plants are usually fast growing and colourful, sometimes garishly so. Think of magenta and orange bougainvilleas screaming for attention alongside scarlet pelargoniums, but perhaps being calmed down by a pale blue plumbago and soft yellow and ochre abutilons. Among the more subtle choices are the gastronomic charms of vines and citrus fruits. These are often associated with the

SHELVES OF FLOWER

Another use of shelves, this time free-standing to create a miniature Hanging Gardens of Babylon where summer flowers, like marguerites, grow alongside evergreen trailers. (p.152)

Mediterranean, and in designing the decor of the conservatory this association can be taken a stage further, with Spanish tiles, terracotta pots and whitewashed walls. Vines and citrus are relatively hardy, sometimes experiencing frosts in their homelands, so will only need a minimum winter temperature of just above freezing which will not involve too great a fuel bill.

At somewhat higher temperatures but still below those required by true tropical plants, a minimum of 10C (50F), it becomes possible to create a yet more exotic ambience. Hibiscuses in a variety of showy oranges, yellows and reds, can flaunt themselves all summer alongside drapes of passion flowers with their extraordinarily complex and colourful flowers. Palms, as has been mentioned in earlier sections, can always be relied upon to accentuate an exotic effect, and daturas, *Brugmansia*, and frangipani, *Plumeria*, to perfume the air with heady tropical scents.

At higher temperatures still, 13C (55F) minimum, it becomes possible to cultivate the true tropicals, like anthuriums, alocasias and *Phalaenopsis* orchids. Such conservatories were not uncommon in Victorian times, but are rare today, partly because of the cost of heating, partly to do with fashion. However, there are now numerous energy-saving devices, double glazing and thermal curtains, for instance, to reduce running costs dramatically. A tropical conservatory will need to be humid for the sake of the plants. But bear in mind that the humidity might not be conducive to human comfort, or a long life for cloth, cane or wooden furnishings.

Conservatories are usually constructed on the sunnier side of a house, but this is not always possible. A shady conservatory still has immense potential, and in very hot summer weather may well seem preferable, a cool and invigorating place away from the stridency of the sun. Most flowering plants will bloom later in the season than in a warmer, brighter place. There are some real sun lovers that might not flower at all without several hours of direct sun a day, the trumpet-shaped pandoreas, podraneas and campsis, for example. Abutilons, with bell-shaped flowers in every shade of red, orange and yellow, and some in white and pink, usually do well in this softer light, and plumbago and jasmines will flower too. If your conservatory is really shady, then consider a ferny grotto, making the most of the wonderful range of foliage that ferns have to offer, including the majestic tree ferns. A cool conservatory will also be ideal for *Lapageria rosea*, a sumptuous climbing lily-relative with red or pink waxy bells in early winter and one of the most beautiful of all indoor plants.

The great thing about conservatories is that they enable you to enjoy plants and gardening in all weathers. When the garden has nothing to offer beyond wind-blown and sodden leaves or a few snowdrops poking their heads above the slush, the conservatory provides a place to sit and relax or potter about. Those days when there are a few rays of winter sun are especially welcome, as a glass structure will heat up remarkably quickly, enticing you to bask, lizard-like, in a comfy chair. You can be surrounded by winter-flowering plants like wattles, *Acacia*, such as the well-known mimosa, or *Acacia dealbata*, with its scented, fluffy yellow flowers, lapagerias and correas, a group of small Australian shrubs. *Correa* 'Mannii' is the best, a non-stop flurry of red bells from Christmas to almost midsummer.

Bulbs do well in conservatories, from tender ones like amaryllis, *Hippeastrum*, and Cape cowslips, *Lachenalia*, to hardy favourites such as hyacinths and daffodils which can be enjoyed at close quarters and in advance of their usual outdoor season. Seasonal pot plants like cyclamen, azaleas and primulas do well in cool conservatories too, better in fact than in the house, because of the lower temperatures and better light.

In summer the conservatory can serve to lead you into the garden, with pots of pelargoniums, lilies, begonias, verbenas and marguerites, *Argyranthemum*, blurring the division between both house and conservatory, and conservatory and garden. Dining *al fresco* is a delight but a slightly chill breeze can all too often turn it into an ordeal, which is where the conservatory can come to the rescue. Remember too when planning to entertain, that some of the finest scents will be at their best at night. Indeed the sumptuously musky night-flowered jessamine, *Cestrum nocturnum*, and the almost overpowering perfume of datura only release their fragrance under cover of darkness (in fact the scent is narcotic and for safety's sake daturas in flower should always be placed by an open door or in the garden – never in a confined space indoors).

Soon you will become entranced by the whole new dimension of gardening that conservatories open up, and the structure becomes frustratingly small. The imagination must be satisfied by putting plants wherever possible. Utilize the wall space with shelves where small and trailing plants can be stacked above each other. Hanging baskets, pots fixed to walls, and climbers that take up little horizontal space are further strategies to fit as much in as possible. My own conservatory is 2.5 by 1.5 metres (8 by 5 feet) with a population of around fifty varieties, yet still has space for two chairs. Conservatories offer far more scope for imaginative planting than the house. So whether you are primarily interested in having a few plants to add interest to an extension, or want to create a thickly planted indoor garden, the possibilities are equally alluring and exciting.

FLYING SAUCERS

Some Art Deco lamps make excellent and imaginative containers for trailing pelargoniums. Although far less elegant, hanging baskets would serve the same purpose just as well. (p.152)

Once a Station Platform

*This remarkable conservatory occupies what was the
station platform, the station itself having been converted
into a house. During summer the doors are flung wide
open, to provide ventilation and to link the house to
the garden, formerly the railway track. (p.153)*

ONE'S OWN JUNGLE

Opposite. *Exotic climbers, Spanish moss – the trailing air plant* Tillandsia *– orchids, plumbago and the climbing African lily* Gloriosa, *create a* *haze of luxuriant vegetation in a west-facing conservatory. It is a great place in which to lie back and dream of a tropical paradise! (p.153)*

FACE THE SETTING SUN

Above. *A variegated abutilon, pelargoniums, spider plants and other species that tolerate temperatures to just above freezing, make this conservatory an* *economical one to heat. It faces west, which means that it will not become too hot, and makes the perfect place to unwind at the end of the day. (p.153)*

PLENTY TO LOOK AT

Right. *A wide range of plants occupy this large conservatory and, together, offer year-round interest and pleasure – cooling lush greenery in summer and the reassuring presence of flourishing plant life in winter. The dwarf banana on the right, in particular, does much to help create an exotic ambience. (p.154)*

DINE IN STYLE

Above. *Conservatories are popular as dining areas, although a fair bit of space is needed to accommodate furniture as well as plants. Notice how the central pillar is used to provide a focus for a grouping of several plants in pots, as well as a support for climbers. (p.154)*

MINIATURE MEDITERRANEAN

Opposite. *Palms, citrus, oleander and scrambling bougainvillea fill a pool-side corner and provide an appropriately Mediterranean atmosphere. Such plants have a long season of flowering, especially if they can* *be given good light and adequate heat throughout the year, as is the case around this indoor swimming pool housed in a conservatory. All of them will, however, survive the winter at lower temperatures. (p.155)*

THE VIEW AT THE DEEP END

Above. *These magnificent-sized specimen plants make all the difference to the atmosphere around this pool. They all require, and receive, good light to produce the strong growth* *needed to keep their shape and colour. It is possible that some plants are affected by the chlorine in swimming pool water, so care needs to be taken when making a selection. (p.155)*

FLOURISHING VINE

Opposite. *This vine is actually rooted in the ground outside the conservatory, where it is much easier to provide the rich growing conditions it requires. It has been* *trained in through a hole in the wall, and, once inside, the leafy vine does a useful job in providing shade during the hottest summer months. (p.156)*

ALWAYS COLOURFUL

Above. *Pelargoniums are one of the most successful of all indoor plants, and deservedly so as they are capable of flowering every day of the year. One of the* *advantages of a conservatory is that it provides enough light to enable such plants to flower through the winter without getting too 'leggy'. (p.155)*

Part Three

PRACTICAL MATTERS

'Oh, I'm not good with house plants, I always kill them.' How often I hear people say this, even those successful at gardening outside. As we have seen in Part Two, the key is sensitivity to the needs of plants and the realization that they are totally dependent on you. Roots encased in a pot, house plants rely on you for every drop of water and nutrient, and are at the mercy of whatever the mini-climate of your home subjects them too, which may be radically different to what they are used to in the wild.

Plants indoors should be treated as individuals; it's no good going around with a can sloshing the same amount of water onto every plant all on the same day; some will get too much and others too little. Nor is it any good putting a plant 'where it looks nice' regardless of its needs; the position has to suit for it to flourish. Learn about the requirements of each variety, and then observe carefully how each plant responds to your care — trial and error is an important part of indoor gardening.

TROPICAL COMFORT

A warm and humid atmosphere enables a variety of different tropical foliage plants to flourish in this conservatory. The grapefruit tree in the pot comes in during winter, but is put out in the garden for the summer. (p.156)

There are certain basic requirements to consider when caring for all indoor plants and I have outlined these below. As space does not allow me to deal with every house plant individually, I suggest you also refer to one of the A to Z type books recommended on page 156.

LIGHT

As this subject has been dealt with in some detail on pages 39 to 79, I will only add some general points here. Light has a marked effect on the appearance and shape of a plant, although this may take months or, in the case of slow-growing palms, years to show. Too much light, and some plants, especially those from humid forest floor environments like calatheas and marantas, will suffer bleached and scorched leaves. Too little, and young leaves become pale and wan, and new growth thin and stretched, especially in the case of succulents and fast-growers like abutilons. All plants grow towards the light which can result in a lop-sided appearance unless they are turned occasionally.

The key to getting the light right is to keep a constant eye on changes in the colour and habit of new growth, and if necessary to be prepared to move plants around to find better places for them. Slower growing kinds like palms and *Ficus* can tick over in a place that is too dark for healthy new growth, but if placed in the light for several months, they can be encouraged to put out some fresh and healthy leaves. During winter, many shade-lovers, particularly ferns, can be moved to sunnier places, and vice versa. See pages 71 to 74.

TEMPERATURE

Many house plants grow naturally at temperatures higher than they normally receive in the home. Consequently high temperatures alone are not a problem for most house plants, although the conditions that often accompany them are: low humidity and rapid drying out. The exceptions are those plants which come from cooler climates like ivies and many seasonal flowering plants like cyclamen.

Along with lack of light, low temperatures are a major limiting factor to what can be grown. Centrally heated houses are ideal for many tropical and subtropical plants like African violets, figs and philodendrons. Homes that aren't centrally heated or are kept cool are less congenial to these plants, although species from cooler climes such as most maidenhair ferns, *Cissus*, aspidistra, cacti and succulents will be more successful.

I do feel that many indoor gardening books underestimate the ability of many tropical plants to cope with relatively low temperatures. For example, I have several *Calathea* species growing at 10-15C (50-60F) during winter, when they are supposed to need 15-20C (60-70F). It is often possible to grow plants at 5 or even 10 degrees Celsius (9 or 18 degrees Fahrenheit) below the normally recommended winter minimum. My experience of growing tropical plants in rather bohemian conditions is that they grow steadily in summer and cease growing in winter, when the trick is to keep them ticking over without too much deterioration, which usually amounts to a certain amount of leaf drop. By spring some look a little sad, but warmer temperatures start them into growth and recovery. Flowering tropicals, like *Phalaenopsis* orchids and anthuriums, need a steady 13C (55F) absolute minimum otherwise flowers will definitely suffer.

Temperature fluctuations are harmful to plants - such as being in rooms heated for the evening but kept cool for the rest of the day, or, worst of all, being left on windowsills with the curtains drawn behind them at night so they chill against the glass. If these conditions prevail, cacti and succulents might be your best bet; as desert plants they are used to such extremes.

HUMIDITY

Many indoor plants originate from places of considerably higher humidity than they will ever experience indoors. Anthuriums relish a steaminess that we would find intolerable, but as with temperature such tropical plants survive at lower humidity than they are used to. Dry air is rarely a problem in cool rooms, but with central heating the air may be harmfully dry, causing leaves to develop brown and crisp edges. Dry air problems are worst in regions which experience very cold winters where the moisture content of the air becomes very low. When heated such atmospheres become desiccating; harmful to human as well as plant health. For tropical rain forest plants like philodendrons, orchids and calatheas, high humidity is essential, especially if they have thin leaves. Many ferns, maidenhairs especially, are also sensitive to dry air.

Certain places should be avoided, except perhaps for cacti; the vicinity of radiators, strong lights and older television sets are all notorious for producing a blast of hot dry air. If dry air is a problem a microclimate can be created around sensitive plants. Group them together on gravel in a tray filled with water. The water will evaporate creating a moister atmosphere for the plants. The bottom of the pots must be above the water level otherwise the compost will become waterlogged.

Use a fine spray gun to mist particularly sensitive or valued plants and as a means of watering epiphytes that absorb moisture through their leaves - such as air plants and stag's horn ferns, *Platycerium*. The aerial roots of many orchids also appreciate a regular misting.

WATERING

This is the most frequent operation and the results of failure tend to be more dramatic than mishaps in other areas of cultivation. Consistent overwatering results in soggy compost, preventing roots from breathing, causing their death and decay. Underwatering puts plants under stress, opening them up to attack from pests and diseases. Consistent underwatering can lead to the compost, particularly peat-based compost, drying out and shrinking away from the side of the pot. Fortunately modern proprietary composts often contain a wetting agent to reduce the danger of this happening, otherwise the pot will need to be soaked in a bucket of water for several hours in order to rewet the compost.

The frequency of watering depends on the season, the type of plant, its location and how much its roots have filled the pot. In summer, plants are actively growing and need more water than when they are resting, which most do in winter. The warmer their environment the more water they need. Sunny conservatories are the extreme case where plants need daily watering through much of summer. During winter when growth is reduced, many plants need water less than once a week, although a few sunny days can rapidly dry out plants by windows. Plants with root-filled pots have reduced the capacity of the compost to hold reserves of water and so will need more frequent watering than those recently repotted.

For water requirements there are, broadly speaking, three categories of plants, together with orchids and bromeliads which are a law unto themselves. First (1) there are those species which should be kept evenly moist; crotons and anthuriums are examples needing water at the very first signs of drying out, although in winter some drying should be allowed. Fast growers with thin leaves, often plants grown for their flowers such as busy lizzies, pelargoniums and argyranthemums, also need a lot of water when actively growing. In winter, keep them much drier, particularly if their environment is cool, as these plants have a tendency to rot in cold, damp conditions.

The second (2), and probably largest, category are those plants that should be allowed to begin to dry out a little before watering - African violets, streptocarpus and most climbers, for instance. In winter, especially if the plants are in the cool, they can be allowed to get quite dry before watering.

The third category is made up of drought-tolerant plants - cacti, succulents, yuccas and ponytail palms, for example. They do need water though! In fact, when in active growth they benefit from being watered whenever they dry out. During winter they are very sensitive to excess water around their roots and it should be given only to prevent excessive withering. This may mean they are kept completely dry.

HOLIDAY TIMES

Going away for holidays can be a real nightmare to keen indoor gardeners. There are really two possibilities: either trust a friend or neighbour and train them well (and risk souring relations if things go wrong!) or adopt some sort of automatic watering system. There are all sorts of sophisticated devices for automated waterings (and which don't rely on computers), these are of particular use to conservatory owners. Capillary matting is one of the simplest and cheapest for general house plant use, but it requires a lot of fiddling, in my experience, to get it working reliably. Therefore you should set the plants on the matting, following the instructions, about a week in advance of departure and make sure that it works effectively. One of the most common problems is that the compost in the pots is not in contact with the matting via the holes in the bottom of the pot. One of the main reasons for this is the habit of 'crocking' pots, see 'Compost and Repotting', below.

FEEDING

A plant in a pot has only limited reserves of nutrients available to it, which makes supplementary feeding essential. Most foliage plants will not need feeding until a year after being repotted, but fast-growing flowering varieties benefit from regular feeding throughout the growing season. The lazy way to feed is to use pellets or sticks, which are inserted into the compost to release nutrients over a period of several months to a year. Otherwise I favour organic feeds, based on seaweed or manure. Buy a brand specified for house plants or for general use, and follow the instructions carefully. Flowering plants benefit from a high potash formulation found in tomato fertilizers.

As a general rule, feed little and often rather than infrequent large quantities. Slow-growers, like many cacti, succulents and bromeliads, are best fed at half the recommended strength, as weak growth can result from overfeeding. Orchids and bonsai have particular requirements and feeds developed specifically for them should be used.

COMPOSTS AND REPOTTING

Plants need repotting if they begin to look starved with yellowing foliage and slow growth, drying out frequently with the compost appearing solid with roots. How often you need to repot depends on the rate of growth of the plant - some palms surviving for years in the same pot - and on how fast you want it to grow. Many species could be repotted every year, but unless you want them to grow through the roof, this can be put off for a year in the case of foliage plants and if you increase feeding. Alternatively 'top dress', which means removing the top few centimetres of compost and replacing it with fresh.

Repot plants in containers less than 10 cm (4 in) in diameter into pots approximately 2-4 cm (1 in) larger; for those in bigger pots, go up 4-6 cm (3 in) in diameter. To encourage young fast- growing flowering plants, like pelargoniums or abutilons, to form large specimens as soon as possible, repot into 20-cm (8-in) pots or larger.

One of the old rules of repotting plants was to put broken bits of pots or stones at the bottom of pots, supposedly to improve drainage. Research now shows that this is unnecessary, and makes watering via capillary matting quite impossible. The only exceptions might be large containers with few or no drainage holes, or orchids.

Drainage is important; roots have to breathe, which they cannot do in waterlogged compost. This is why pots with plenty of holes in the bottom are really important. Bear this in mind when selecting new containers; those that look the most attractive are not always the most practical. Of course, this makes it vital that pots always have a saucer underneath to catch excess water, and it is also vital that this saucer is not always awash. A little extra water will soon dry up, but a constant puddle . . . and you might as well grow the plant in a bucket! Utility plant pots are often concealed inside more attractive ornamental pots or other containers, with no drainage holes. A frequent cause of watering problems in my experience is that the contents of these outer pots are never checked; water can build up inside them and flood the root system.

Composts specially designed for house plants are now widely available, but often have the disadvantage of being made from peat, which is not only environmentally damaging to harvest but too light to support tall, top-heavy plants. A heavier soil-based compost can be used instead. John Innes No.2 is best for most house plants, although fast-growing flowering varieties will benefit from the higher level of nutrients in John Innes No.3. For plants like African violets or streptocarpus that are sensitive to too much water, it is worth improving the drainage by mixing four parts compost with one part, by volume, grit or, best of all, perlite, a kind of geological popcorn which does wonders aerating composts and promoting healthy root growth. Cacti and succulents prefer a mixture of three parts John Innes No.1 to one part grit or perlite.

TRAINING, SHAPING AND TIDYING UP

Some plants stay compact and never seem to need trimming. Taller growing woody plants like scheffleras, figs or Ficus, and dracaenas can become leggy and ungainly with age. To prevent this pinch out the growing tip of the plant before it gets too tall to encourage side branching. Dracaenas can be cut hard back into mature wood and they will resprout, but for many woody plants, including figs, this cannot be guaranteed, so such hard pruning should be avoided if possible. Instead, encourage plants to grow straight and, if they threaten to become lopsided, tie to a cane.

Fast-growing conservatory plants like oleanders, bougainvilleas, plumbago and abutilons can be cut back hard into mature wood, preferably in autumn or after flowering, and they will produce young and vigorous new growth, even from the base. Climbers and trailers can become untidy, especially the faster growing ones like tradescantias and Cissus. These can be cut back to encourage new growth towards the bottom of the plant.

Remove all dead leaves and stems as they can become a source of diseases especially in cooler winter conditions. Dust can build up rapidly on leaves, reducing a plant's ability to 'breathe' and to receive light. Clean large smooth leaves, such as Draceana and Monstera, with a damp cloth or proprietary leaf wipes. Hairy leaves, like those of African violets and columneas, are best gently brushed with an old, soft toothbrush.

PESTS AND DISEASES

These are not too much of a problem in the home, but can lead to plagues of biblical proportions in conservatories. Chemical sprays are now rightly regarded with suspicion, especially in the home, and on a small scale insect invaders can be removed by hand. Insecticidal soap sprays are extremely safe, however, and effective if the foliage is thoroughly soaked. Among the conventional sprays, the safest are those containing plant-derived chemicals, like pyrethrum and derris, or synthetic versions, like permethrin. Even so you must read the instructions carefully, store them well away from children and pets, and never apply them near fish. Be aware that some people can develop allergies to the safest chemicals.

The plagues of whiteflies, red spider mites and scale insects that can reduce conservatory owners to tears are best dealt with by means of biological controls, which use natural insect predators to eat or parasitize the pests. They are relatively expensive but can save much time otherwise spent on spraying. They can only be bought by mail order; see page 157 for stockists or consult the gardening press.

Diseases usually mean fungal problems often caused by incorrect care, over or under watering. Botrytis, or grey mould, is the worst problem, but usually only in conservatories in cold damp winter weather. It is best prevented by watering as little as possible in such conditions, removing all dead material and keeping the air moving by ventilation or use of an electric fan.

CONSERVATORIES

Conservatories tend to be much hotter than the house in summer when ventilation is vital for the comfort of people and plants. Give some thought to security, as it is important to ensure that intruders cannot sneak in with the cooling breezes. Shading for sunny conservatories should be considered, either in the form of blinds or by training vigorous climbing plants like passion flowers to do the job.

Free-flowering, vigorous growers will need frequent watering and feeding through the summer, and close attention should be paid to the threat of insect pests from spring onwards (see above). By the autumn many conservatory plants will have grown enormous and may need ruthless cutting back before the onset of winter. From then until spring - be aware of the danger of botrytis (see above).

KEY TO PLANT INFORMATION

Plant height A guide to the *eventual* height is given after each plant name as follows:
Small: under 30 cm (1 ft);
Medium: under 1m (3 ft 3in);
Tall: more than 1m (3ft 3in).

Flowering season This is given for plants grown for their flowers. All-year denotes flowering potential at any season (not flowering non-stop); growing several plants and different cultivars will often ensure that there is always at least one in flower.

Position Refers to how much light the plants need.

Temperature The figure given indicates minimum winter temperature; in fact most will survive short periods below this, see also page 134.

Humidity Tolerates dry air: suitable for cacti, succulents and other desert plants.
Dry air harmful: problems might arise, especially at higher temperatures (above 25C/77F).
Average: ambient humidity is nearly always sufficient.
Reasonable: plants require relatively high humidity, and benefit from being grown over gravel trays or regularly misted.

Watering Normal requirements: plants are fairly easy going about their water needs, either watering category (1) or (2) - see page 135. The water requirements of bromeliads and orchids have been discussed in their relevant sections, see pages 99-102 and 109-111 respectively.

Feeding Normal requirements: plants benefit from feeding with a proprietary house plant fertilizer, used according to the manufacturer's instructions, during their period of active growth which is usually between late spring and later summer. See also page 135.

A Windowful of Colour	Page 2

1. *Streptocarpus* 'Joanna' (small, summer)
2. *Streptocarpus* 'Sandra' (small, summer)
3. *Streptocarpus* 'Heidi' (small, summer)
4. *Streptocarpus* 'Albatross' (small, summer)
5. *Streptocarpus* 'Cynthia' (small, summer)

Position good indirect light, perhaps a few hours of direct sun a day
Temperature 8C (46F) min.
Humidity average

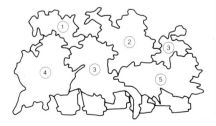

Watering and feeding dry out a little before watering; normal feeding
Comments aphids can be a problem. Propagate by leaf cuttings.

Dynamic Contrast	Page 6

1. *Ficus longifolia* (tall)
2. *Chrysalidocarpus lutescens* (tall)
3. *Strelitzia nicolaii* (tall)
4. *Gardenia jasminoides* (medium, summer)
5. *Philodendron domesticum* (*P. hastatum*) (climber)

Position good indirect light, perhaps a few hours of sun
Temperature 10C (50F) min.
Humidity dry air harmful
Watering and feeding normal
Comments gardenia prefers a lime free compost and water.

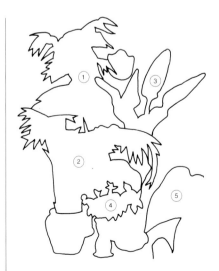

Making the Most of the Sun — Page 20

1. *Jasminum azoricum* (climber, spring)
2. *Pisonia umbellifera* (P. brunoniana) 'Variegata' (tall)
3. *Schefflera (Heptapleurum) arboricola* (tall)
4. *Coffea arabica* (tall)
5. *Billbergia* 'Fantasia' (medium, summer)
6. *Dieffenbachia × bausei* (medium)
7. *Musa velutina* (medium)
8. *Neoregelia spectabilis* (medium, all-year)
9. *Dieffenbachia* 'Camille' (medium)
10. *Begonia rex* 'Silver Greenheart' (medium)
11. *Jasminum polyanthum* (climber, winter)

Position good indirect light; taller plants at front enjoy some direct sun, those shaded by them prefer indirect light
Temperature 10C (50F) min., 1 and 11 down to 0C (32F)
Humidity dry air harmful
Watering and feeding normal; 8 and 9, see bromeliads pages 99–100
Comments as 1 and 11 will only flower if kept cool over winter, move to a cool light room in early autumn.

Form and Fragrance — Page 22

From left to right:
1. *Solandra maxima* (tall, autumn)
2. *Cattleya* hybrid (small, all-year)
3. *Vriesea* species (medium, all-year)
4. *Hedychium coronarium* (tall, summer)

Position good indirect light
Temperature 10C (50F) min.; 2 13C (55F) min.
Humidity dry air harmful
Watering and feeding normal; 2 and 3 (a bromeliad), need careful watering and feeding at half normal strength, see pages 109 and 99-100 respectively
Comments 2 requires orchid compost.

Tabletop Tree — Page 23

Sageretia thea (small)

Position good indirect light
Temperature cooler than average room temperature, 8C (46F) min.in winter

Humidity dry air harmful
Watering and feeding normal watering; use proprietary bonsai feed
Comments refer to a bonsai manual for guidance on training, pruning and special care.

Poem in Brown and Blue — Page 24

Ludisia discolor (small)

Position soft indirect light
Temperature 13C (55F) min.
Humidity reasonable humidity
Watering and feeding see page 109
Comments use orchid compost for repotting.

Stairway and Sunset — Page 25

From left to right:
1. × *Fatshedera lizei* (tall)
2. *Elettaria cardamonum* (medium)
3. *Fatsia japonica* (tall)

Position light shade, or brighter, indirect light
Temperature avoid high temperatures; 1 and 3 are hardy outdoors; 2 down to 0C (32F)
Humidity average
Watering and feeding normal
Comments pinch back 1 occasionally to keep it shrubby, or train as a climber; if 1 or 3 get too big, plant in the garden; 2 can be divided.

GROWING TOGETHER
Indoor plants in groups

Pick of the Best — Page 26

1. *Nephrolepis exaltata* 'Smithii' (small)
2. *Streptocarpus* 'Heidi' (small, summer)
3. *Pelargonium graveolens* 'Variegatum' (medium)
4. *Peperomia caperata* (small)
5. *Sedum sieboldii* (small, summer)
6. *Pilea peperomioides* (small)
7. *Asparagus densiflorus* Sprengeri Group (medium)

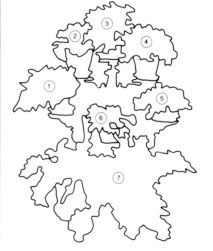

Position good indirect light; 3 prefers some sun; 1, 6, 7 tolerate low light
Temperature 5 is hardy; 1, 3, 7 3C (37F) min.; 2, 4, 6 8C (46F) min.
Humidity dry air harmful
Watering and feeding normal; allow 2, 4 and 6 to dry a little before watering
Comments a temporary display, but these plants will grow together satisfactorily in this position.

Shades of Purple	Page 28

From left to right:
1. *Begonia rex* 'Vesuvius' (medium)
2. *Peperomia fraseri* (small)
3. *Tradescantia pallida (Setreasea purpurea)* (medium, summer)

Position good indirect light
Temperature 10C (50F) min.
Humidity normal
Watering and feeding normal; allow 2 to dry out before watering
Comments 3 does well in brighter light, and copes with lower temperatures.

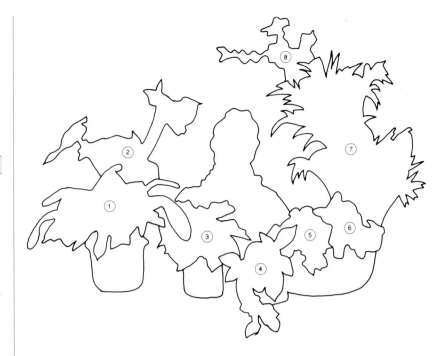

A Corner of Elegance	Page 29

1. *Sanchezia nobilis* (tall)
2. *Schefflera digitata (Dizygotheca elegantissima)* (tall)
3. *Schefflera actinophylla* (tall)
4. *Begonia luxurians* (tall, summer)

Position good indirect light, possibly some direct sun
Temperature 10C (50F) min.
Humidity reasonable
Watering and feeding normal
Comments 2 may lose its leaves if conditions change suddenly. All can get leggy with time and should be pinched out to encourage branching or cut back if they become too tall. Mealy bug and red spider mite can be a problem.

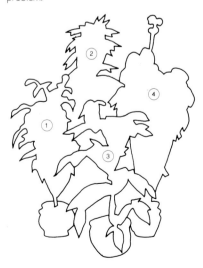

A Lively Bunch	Page 31

1. *Strelitzia nicolaii* (tall)
2. *Pandorea jasminoides* (climber, summer)
3. *Solenostemon (Coleus)* 'Paisley Shawl' (medium)
4. Zonal pelargonium (medium, all-year)
5. *Chlorophytum comosum* 'Vittatum' (medium)

Position sun for several hours a day
Temperature 5C (40F) min.; 4 and 5 down to -2C (28F).
Humidity dry air harmful
Watering and feeding normal
Comments 2 needs very good light to flower; keep 3 pinched back to encourage bushy growth; keep 4 on the dry side in winter, especially if kept cool.

Cool and Classical	Page 32

1. *Aechmea fasciata* (small, all-year)
2. *Anthurium andreanum* (medium, all-year)
3. *Begonia rex* 'Salamander' (medium)
4. *Episcia cupreata* 'Chocolate Soldier' (small, summer)
5. *Begonia rex* 'Kathleyana' (medium)
6. *Calathea stromata* (small)
7. *Phoenix roebelenii* (tall)
8. *Jasminum polyanthum* (climber, winter)

Position light shade to good indirect light; 7 and 8 prefer some sunlight
Temperature 10C (50F) min.; 7 down to 5C (40F)
Humidity dry air harmful
Watering and feeding normal; allow 1, 3, 4, 5 and 7 to dry out slightly before watering
Comments 8 needs good light and cool winter temperatures (down to 0C/32F) to encourage flowering.

Contrasting Threesome	Page 34

From left to right:
1. *Schefflera digitata (Dizygotheca elegantissima)* 'Castor' (medium)
2. *Solenostemon (Coleus)* 'Carnival' (medium)
3. *Rhapis excelsa* (medium)

Position good indirect light
Temperature 10C (50F) min.
Humidity dry air harmful
Watering and feeding normal
Comments 1 is very sensitive to sudden temperature and other changes; 2 will take stronger light and temperatures down to 5C (40F); 3 also does well in shade.

Variety and Balance — *Page 35*

1. *Elettaria cardamomum* (medium)
2. *Codiaeum variegatum* 'Gloriosa' (medium)
3. *Solenostemon (Coleus)* 'Rustic Splendour' (medium)
4. *Calathea zebrina* (medium)
5. *Cissus rhombifolia* 'Ellen Danica' (climbing or trailing)

Position good indirect light; 1, 4 and 5 tolerate shade; 3 does best with some sun
Temperature 12C (54F) min.; 1, 3 and 5 can go down to 5C (40F).
Humidity dry air harmful
Watering and feeding normal; 2 is very sensitive to drying out during the warmer months
Comments 2 can be troubled by mealy bug; 3 needs frequent pinching out to keep bushy; 5 can be grown as a climber.

Once a Warehouse — *Page 36*

1. *Polyscias fruticosa* (tall)
2. *Scindapsus aureus* (trailer)
3. *Asplenium nidus phyllitidis* (medium)
4. *Hippeastrum* cultivar (medium, winter)

Position good indirect light
Temperature 10C (50F) min.
Humidity dry air harmful
Watering and feeding normal; 4 usually goes dormant several months after flowering, then keep dry until autumn
Comments 1 can suffer leaf drop if conditions change suddenly or the air is dry; 2 can be grown as a climber; 2 and 3 tolerate shade.

Winter Scene — *Page 37*

1. *Zamia floridana* (medium)
2. *Farfugium tussilagineum* 'Aureomaculatum' (medium)
3. *Farfugium tussilagineum* 'Argenteum' (medium)
4. *Zamia furfuracea* (medium)
5. *Ficus deltoidea diversifolia* (small, winter berries)

Position good indirect light
Temperature 5 10C (50F) min.; 1 to 4 down to 5C (40F); 2 and 3 0C (32F) min.
Humidity average
Watering and feeding normal; 1 and 4 need little water in winter
Comments 2 and 3 are best stood, or planted, outside in summer; turn 5 occasionally to keep the rounded shape.

BASKING IN THE SUN
Plants for bright light

A Bold Statement — *Page 38*

Archontophoenix cunninghamiana (tall)

Position good light, several hours sunlight a day
Temperature 10C (50F) min.
Humidity reasonable
Watering and feeding normal.

Soaking up the Sun — *Page 40*

1. *Yucca elephantipes* (tall)
2. *Begonia* Lorraine hybrid (small, spring-autumn)

3. *Plectranthus oertendahlii* (medium)
4. *Sansevieria trifasciata* 'Laurentii' (medium)
5. *Astrophytum ornatum* (small)
6. *Sedum* species (small)
7. *Fenestraria aurantiaca* (small, summer)
8. *Crassula argentea* (medium, summer)
9. *Mammilaria evermanniana* (small, summer)
10. *Lobivia winterana* (small)
11. *Ceropegia linearis* ssp. *woodii* (small)
12. *Euphorbia obesa* (small)
13. *Adromischus cooperi* (small)
14. *Ferocactus emoryi* (small)
15. *Mammilaria elongata* (small, summer)
16. *Opuntia tuna* 'Monstrosa' (small)
17. *Mammilaria plumosa* (small, summer)
18. *Ficus benjamina* (tall)

Position direct sunlight for much of the day
Temperature 5C (40F) min.; some cacti will tolerate less
Humidity tolerant of dry air
Watering and feeding water succulents whenever they dry out in summer, monthly in winter; apply a balanced feed at half strength. 2, 3, 18 are not succulent so feed and water normally
Comments grow cacti and succulents in a low-nutrient compost such as John Innes No. 1, with added grit to assist good drainage; stand outside in summer to ensure firm and healthy growth; watch out for mealy bug on cacti and succulents.

Flowers for Winter	Page 41

1. *Begonia* x *corallina* 'Lucerna' (medium, summer and autumn)
2. *Ananas comosus* (medium)

3. *Kalanchoe blossfeldiana* cultivars (small, all-year)
4. *Schlumbergera (Zygocactus) bridgesii* (medium, late autumn-spring)
5. *Iresine herbstii* (medium)
6. *Citrus* cultivar (medium, winter)
7. *Cyclamen persicum* miniature cultivars (small, autumn-spring)
8. *Aloe arborescens* (medium)

Position sunlight for much of the day
Temperature 10C (50F); 6, 7, 8 can go lower
Humidity normal
Watering and feeding normal; 3 and 7 liable to fungal rots so water with care
Comments keep 3 dry and cool for a month after flowering. Stand 7 outside in a cool place for the summer and allow to go dormant; bring inside in autumn when it starts into growth and repot. Scale insect can be a problem on 6.

Plants for Modern Living	Page 42

1. *Yucca elephantipes* (tall)
2. *Ficus elastica* (tall)
3. *Beaucarnia (Nolina) elegans* (tall)
4. *Philodendron erubescens* 'Burgundy' (climber)

Position 1 and 3 in sunlight for several hours a day; 2 and 4 good indirect light
Temperature 2 and 4 10C (50F) min.; 1 and 3 5C (40F) min.
Humidity 2 and 4 reasonable; 1 and 3 more tolerant of dry air
Watering and feeding 2 and 4 normal; 1 and 3 fairly drought tolerant, but to do well need normal watering in summer

Comments 2 can look awkward with age, this one has been pinched out at some stage to encourage branching; 4 has been allowed to trail but in time it will become too long and gangly to be attractive, so train it up wires or a moss pole for a better long-term solution.

Impressive Specimens	Page 43

From left to right:
1. *Myricaria cauliflora* (medium)
2. *Dracaena fragrans* (tall)
3. *Hibiscus rosa-sinensis* cultivar (tall, spring-autumn)

Position sunlight for several hours a day
Temperature 1 and 2 5C (40F) min.; 3 8C (46F) min.
Humidity dry air harmful
Watering and feeding normal watering; allow 2 to dry out slightly between waterings in the winter. Feed 1 with a proprietary bonsai fertilizer. Feed 3 regularly using a tomato feed to stimulate flowering during the growing season
Comments bonsai need careful pruning, refer to a specialist book. As 3 is grown as a standard, remove any growth from the base of the trunk and cut back branches that grow out sideways to preserve the shape.

Plants and Masks	Page 44

1. *Echinocactus grusonii* (medium)
2. *Euphorbia pseudocactus* (medium)
3. *Aloe eru (A. camperi)* (medium)
4. *Dracaena draco* (tall)
5. *Pandanus veitchii* (tall)

Position sunlight for at least several hours a day
Temperature 5C (40F) min.; 5 needs min. of 10C (50F)
Humidity tolerant of dry air
Watering and feeding normal watering in summer, very little in winter; feed 4 and 5 normally, 1, 2 and 3 at half strength
Comments watch out for mealy bug on succulents.

Desert Fish   Page 44

1. *Echinopsis* (*Lobivia*) species (small)
2. *Opuntia microdasys* 'Albospina' (small)
3. *Mammillaria schiedeana* (small)
4. *lMammillaria elongata* (small)

Position sunlight for several hours a day
Temperature 5C (40F) min.
Humidity tolerant of dry air
Watering and feeding careful watering in summer, very little in winter. Since there is no drainage in this container, ensure that water does not accumulate at the bottom. Little feeding necessary
Comments watch out for mealy bug.

An Autumn Rarity   Page 45

1. *Vallota speciosa* (*Cyrtanthus elatus*) (medium, autumn)
2. *Echeveria shaviana* hybrid (small)
3. *Echeveria glauca* cultivar (small)
4. *Echeveria* cultivar (small)

Position several hours of sun a day
Temperature 5C (40F) min.
Humidity dry air harmful to 1; 2, 3 and 4 tolerate dry air
Watering and feeding cool and on the dry side in winter to keep almost dormant; normal in summer
Comments do not repot 1 until potbound (crowded with bulbs).

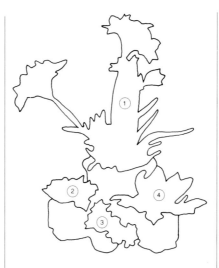

A Tree Indoors   Page 46

Pithecellobium flexicaule (tall)

Position sunlight for several hours a day
Temperature 5C (40F) min.
Humidity dry air harmful
Watering and feeding normal
Comments be prepared to prune if it gets too tall.

Spikes and Curves   Page 47

From left to right:
1. *Sansevieria* 'Bantel's Sensation' (medium)
2. *Sansevieria cylindrica* (medium)
3. *Beaucamea recurvata* (*Nolina tuberculata*) (tall)

Position sunlight for much of the day
Temperature 5C (40F) min.
Humidity tolerant of dry air
Watering and feeding water only when drying out, very infrequently in winter; normal feeding.

Colour in the Leaves   Page 48

From left to right:
1. *Ficus elastica* (tall)
2. *Cordyline fruticosa* 'Alborosea' (medium)
3. *Ficus rubiginosa* 'Variegata' (tall)
4. *Strelitzia nicolai* (tall)

Position sunlight for several hours a day, but do well in good indirect light
Temperature 10C (50F) min.
Humidity some tolerance of dry air
Watering and feeding normal
Comments pinch out tips or cut back if plants threaten to get too big; 2 will resprout if cut back.

Degrees of Light   Page 49

1. *Syngonium angustatum* 'Albolineatum' (medium)
2. *Sinningia* (*Rechsteineria*) *cardinalis* (small, summer)
3. Zonal pelargonium (medium, all-year)
4. *Cissus rhombifolia* (climber)

Position see caption
Temperature 10C (50F) min.; 3 and 4 down to 0C (32F)
Humidity 1 reasonable; 2, 3 and 4 average
Watering and feeding normal
Comments allow 2 to go dormant in autumn, keep dry and cool over winter, repot tubers in spring.

Succulents en Masse   Page 50

1. *Senecio* (*Kleinia*) *fulgens* (medium)
2. *Rhipsalis capilliformis* (medium)
3. *Senecio serpens* (*Kleinia repens*) (medium)
4. *Aeonium arboreum* 'Atropurpureum' (medium)
5. *Sansevieria trifasciata* 'Laurentii' (medium)
6. *Agave americana* (medium)
7. *Crassula* species (medium?)
8. *Aeonium arboreum* (medium)
9. *Euphorbia xylophylloides* (medium)
10. *Synadenium grantii* 'Rubra' (tall)
11. *Kalanchoe* species (medium)

Position sunlight for at least several hours a day
Temperature 5C (40F) min. although many will take lower
Humidity tolerant of dry air
Watering and feeding be generous with water and feeding during the growing season, but restrict watering in winter to just sufficient to stop withering
Comments in a case like this where there are many plants in one container, cut back vigorous growers or they will elbow slower growing companions out of the way; occasional pruning will also maintain the well-balanced shape of the planting.

Almost a Tree — Page 56

Polyscias scutellaria (tall)

Position good indirect light
Temperature 10C (50F) min.
Humidity dry air harmful
Watering and feeding normal
Comments can be sensitive to sudden changes in conditions.

Swollen Stems of the Desert — Page 51

1. *Pachypodium lamerei* (medium)
2. *Pachypodium* species
3. *Bowiea volubilis* (small)
4. *Ficus petiolaris* (medium)

Position sunlight for several hours a day
Temperature 5C (40F) min.
Humidity tolerant of dry air
Watering and feeding very little in winter, especially if cool; normal at other times.

LIGHT BUT NOT BRIGHT
Soft and subdued light

Variegated Beauty — Page 52

Ficus aspera 'Variegata' (tall)

Position good indirect light
Temperature 12C (54F) min.
Humidity reasonable
Watering and feeding normal
Comments may suffer leaf drop if conditions change suddenly.

Plants and Porcelain — Page 55

1. *Chirita sinensis* (small, summer)
2. *Saintpaulia* 'Granaat' (small all-year)
3. *Saintpaulia* 'Rood' (small all-year)
4. *Saintpaulia* 'Mariska' (small all-year)
5. *Saintpaulia* 'Monica' (small all-year)
6. *Saintpaulia* 'R.E.Beryl' (small all-year)
7. *Saintpaulia* 'Athena' (small all-year)
8. *Begonia hispida* (small, summer)

Position good indirect light
Temperature 12C (54F) min.
Humidity reasonable
Watering and feeding allow to dry slightly before watering; regular feeding will encourage flowering; 8 needs slightly more moisture than the others
Comments African violets are among the most successful plants under artificial light.

Greening the City — Page 57

1. *Ophiopogon jaburan* (medium)
2. *Guzmania lingulata minor* (medium, all-year)
3. *Gardenia augusta* (*G. jasminoides*) 'Fortuniana' (tall, summer)
4. *Gardenia augusta* (*G. jasminoides*) 'Veitchii' (medium, summer)
5. *Cattleya* hybrid (medium, winter)
6. *Zamia floridana* (medium)
7. *Polyscias fruticosa* (tall)

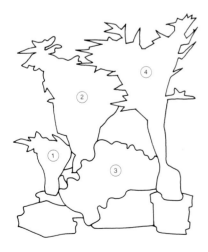

Position good indirect light, some direct sunlight beneficial
Temperature 10C (50F) min.; 12C (54F) min.
Humidity reasonable

Watering and feeding normal; 2 and 5 need careful watering and reduced feeding, see pages 99–100 and 109 respectively.

Comments gardenias have a reputation for being difficult. Survival tricks include keeping the base of the pot in a tray with 2 cm (1 in) of water, and watering with coffee grounds, which helps to keep the compost acid. It is also important not to change their conditions too frequently, and to repot with a lime-free compost.

A Collector's Windowsill	Page 59

1. *Passiflora racemosa* (climber, summer)
2. *Ceropegia linearis* ssp. *woodii* (medium)
3. *Plectranthus oertendahlii* (medium)
4. *Streptocarpus* cultivar (small, summer)
5. *Saintpaulia* 'Erin Colleen' (small, all-year)
6. *Pilea nummulariifolia* (small)
7. *Saintpaulia* 'Ma Gigi' (small, all-year)
8. *Billbergia nutans* (medium, spring)
9. *Saintpaulia* 'Tomahawk' (small, all-year)
10. *Saintpaulia* 'Trail Along' (small, all-year)
11. *Saintpaulia* 'Skagit's Ambassador' (small, all-year)
12. *Begonia* 'Burle Marx' (medium, summer)
13. *Abutilon* cultivar (tall, summer)
14. *Saintpaulia* 'Moonkist'

Position good indirect light; 1, 2, 8 and 13 do best in full sun and may be stood outside in a sheltered spot for summer; 6 thrives in shade
Temperature 8, 13 hardy to -2C (28F); 1, 3, 4 5C (40F) min; the others need a min. of 12C (54F)
Humidity dry air harmful
Watering and feeding 1 and 13 need copious watering and feeding in summer, less so in winter; keep 12 reasonably moist in summer, drier in winter; allow 2 and 3 to dry out slightly after watering, keep fairly dry in winter; water the others only when they begin to dry out. Normal feeding; proprietary African violet feed for 5, 7, 9, 10, 11 to promote a long flowering season.

Cottage Window Colour	Page 60

From left to right:
1. *Streptocarpus* 'Tina' (small, summer)
2. *Streptocarpus* 'Gloria' (small, summer)
3. *Streptocarpus* 'Falling Stars' (small, summer)

Position good indirect light or a few hours of sun; sunlight welcome in winter
Temperature 8C (46F) min.
Humidity normal

Watering and feeding allow to dry out a little before watering, regular feeding during summer will help to maintain flowering
Comments keep greenfly at bay.

Streptocarpus Palette	Page 61

1. *Streptocarpus* 'Ruby' (small, summer)
2. *Streptocarpus* 'Elsie' (small, summer)
3. *Streptocarpus* 'Heidi' (small, summer)
4. *Streptocarpus* 'Beryl' (small, summer)
5. *Streptocarpus* 'Tina' (small, summer)
6. *Streptocarpus* 'Wiesmoor Red' (small, summer)
7. *Streptocarpus* 'Kim' (small, summer)

For position and care see above, 'Cottage Window Colour'.

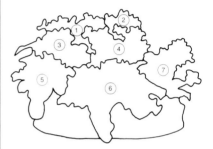

A Leafy Lounge	Page 62

From left to right:
1. *Livistonia chinensis* (tall)
2. *Philodendron erubescens* 'Red Emerald' (climber)
3. *Syngonium podophyllum* (climber)

Position 1 benefits from some direct sun; 2, 3 good indirect light
Temperature 10C (50F) min.; 1 down to 5C (40F)
Humidity dry air harmful
Watering and feeding 1 can dry out a little between waterings; 2 and 3 need constant moisture. Normal feeding
Comments 3 can also be grown on a moss pole.

Beautiful Begonias	Page 63

From left to right:
1. *Begonia fuchsioides* (medium, summer)
2. *Begonia albopicta* (medium, summer)

Position good indirect light, some direct sun is tolerated and beneficial in winter
Temperature 10C (50F) min.
Humidity dry air harmful
Watering and feeding normal; take care in winter if the plants are kept cool, as they rot easily. Normal feeding.

In Solitary Splendour — Page 64

Begonia bowerae 'Tiger' (small)

Position good indirect light, some direct sunlight tolerated
Temperature 5C (40F) min.
Humidity dry air harmful
Watering and feeding normal.

Foliage Forms — Page 65

1. *Tradescantia (Rhoeo) spathacea* (medium)
2. *Begonia bowerae* (small)
3. *Peperomia obtusifolia Magnoliaefolia Group* (small)
4. *Ctenanthe oppenheimiana* 'Tricolor' (medium)
5. *Pilea peperomioides* (small)

Position good indirect light; 1 and 5 do well in shadier conditions and should not receive direct summer sun
Temperature 10C (50F) min.
Humidity dry air harmful
Watering and feeding normal; allow 3 to dry out between waterings.

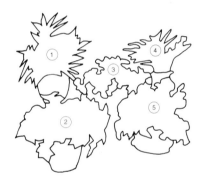

Russet Tones — Page 66

From left to right:
1. *Achimenes* 'Glory' (small, summer)
2. *Aeschynanthus* 'Big Apple' (late summer-winter)

Position good indirect light
Temperature 8C (46F) min.
Humidity dry air harmful
Watering and feeding keep moist in growing season; allow to dry out before watering in winter
Comments dry off achimenes in the autumn and store dry and cool over winter. In spring repot the tiny tubers and start into growth in a warm place (even an airing cupboard) before moving to their summer home. Watch out for greenfly.

Washing up with Flowers — Page 67

From left to right:
1. *Aeschynanthus* 'Bold Venture' (small, summer-autumn)

2. *Nematanthus* 'Black Gold' (medium, summer)
3. 2 × *Kohleria* 'Dark Velvet' (medium, summer)

Position good indirect light
Temperature 8C (46F) min.
Humidity dry air harmful
Watering and feeding keep moist when growing, but allow to dry out before watering in winter. Normal feeding
Comments either treat 3 like achimenes and dry off for winter (see above, 'Russet tones'), or cut back in spring.

Four in One — Page 68

4 × *Pachira aquatica* (tall)

Position good indirect light, happy with some sun
Temperature 10C (50F) min.
Humidity dry air harmful
Watering and feeding normal
Comments keep long growths cut back to maintain rounded shape; good light and frequent turning will also encourage sturdy symmetrical growth.

The Latest Pink — Page 69

Syngonium 'Infra-red' (small)

Position good indirect light, happy with some shade
Temperature 10C (50F) min.
Humidity reasonable
Watering and feeding keep moist in summer, slightly drier in winter; normal feeding.

GREENING THE GLOOM
Plants for shade

Post-Modern Aspidistras — Page 70

Aspidistra elatior (medium)

Position tolerant of any conditions except direct sun
Temperature -2C (28F) min.
Humidity tolerant of dry air
Watering and feeding frequent in summer; reduce in winter, survives drought to some extent. Often neglected, but feed normally for impressive plants
Comments probably the toughest house plant, but can suffer from red spider mite infestation in dry conditions.

A Shady Corner — Page 72

From left to right:
1. *Chamaedorea elegans* (medium)
2. *Nephrolepis exaltata* (medium)

Position light shade; 2 does well in stronger light
Temperature 5C (40F) min.

Humidity average; 2 is more tolerant of dry air than most ferns
Watering and feeding normal.

Skylight Highlight — Page 74

Adiantum raddianum (small)

Position indirect light
Temperature keep cool, below 20C (70F); 0C (32F) min.
Humidity reasonable humidity essential; mist frequently or stand on a wet gravel tray if there is any risk of dry air.
Watering and feeding keep constantly moist but not wet; suffers badly if allowed to dry out. Feed at half normal strength
Comments can be susceptible to greenfly.

Where Eagles Dwell — Page 75

From left to right:
1. *Soleirolia soleirolii* (small)
2. *Pilea cadierei* (small)
3. *Chamaerops costaricana* (medium)

Position light shade or indirect light
Temperature 8C (46F) min.
Humidity dry air harmful
Watering and feeding 1 needs a constantly moist soil; 2 prefers to dry out slightly between waterings. Normal feeding
Comments 1 can be grown with larger plants and allowed to cover the compost.

A Wreath for the Emperor — Page 76

1. *Cissus rhombifolia* (climber)
2. *Asparagus plumosus* (climber)
3. *Dracaena marginata* (medium)
4. *Pteris cretica albolineata* (small)

Position light shade or indirect light
Temperature 5C (40F) min.

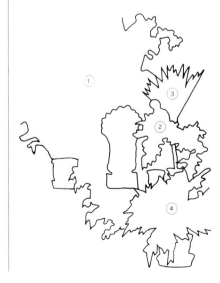

Humidity dry air harmful
Watering and feeding normal
Comments 2 can climb by twining around a support, although it is usually grown as a free-standing plant; 3 can get leggy after a few years - it will resprout if you are brave and cut it back.

Some Like it Damp	Page 77

1. *Pteris cretica longifolia* (medium)
2. *Adiantum hispidulum* (small)
3. *Pteris ensiformis victoriae* (small)
4. *Selaginella kraussiana* (small)

Position light shade; 1, 2, 3 will tolerate indirect light if humidity is maintained
Temperature 5C (40F) min. for 1 and 3; 2 and 4 prefer 10C (50F) min.
Humidity reasonable, especially 4 which is ideally grown in terrariums such as bottle gardens
Watering and feeding keep slightly moist at all times, particularly in summer. Feed at half strength.

Bathroom Jungle	Page 78

1. *Spathiphyllum wallisii* (medium, all-year)
2. *Davallia trichomanoides* (small)
3. *Maranta leuconeura* var. *kerchoveana* (small)
4. *Asplenium bulbiferum* (medium)
5. *Pellaea rotundifolia* (small)
6. *Alocasia macrorrhiza* (medium)

Position shade or indirect light, no sun
Temperature 10C (50F) min.; 3 will take a little lower; 2 and 4 down to 0C (32F); 6 prefers 12C (54F).
Humidity dry air harmful
Watering and feeding keep evenly moist in summer; dry out slightly before watering in winter
Comments watch out for scale on 2, 4 and 5.

Matching the Paintwork	Page 79

1. *Polypodium* (*Phlebodium*) *aureum* (medium)
2. *Ficus pumila* (climber)
3. *Pteris cretica* 'Wimsettii' (small)
4. *Chamaedorea elegans* (medium)

Position shade or brighter indirect light
Temperature 5C (40F) min.
Humidity reasonable
Watering and feeding evenly moist in summer, dry out slightly before watering in winter
Comments 2 can be grown as a climber.

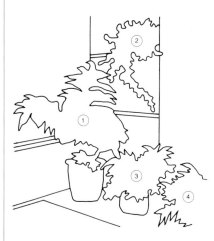

A TOUCH OF THE TROPICS
Keep up the heat

Tropical Decadence	Page 80

1. *Calathea makoyana* (medium)
2. *Spathiphyllum* 'Mauna Loa' (medium)
3. *Calathea veitchiana* (medium)
4. *Ctenanthe oppenheimiana* (medium)
5. *Asplenium nidus* (medium)
6. *Anthurium veitchii* (medium, all-year)

Position shade or brighter but indirect light
Temperature 13C (55F) min., do well above 18C (65F); 4, 5 and 6 tolerate down to 10C (50F)
Humidity reasonable, especially if warm

Watering and feeding keep moist in summer; dry out before watering in winter particularly if cool. Normal feeding
Comments take great care to avoid damaging young growth of 5.

Music with Plants	Page 83

1. *Phalaenopsis* hybrid (medium, all-year)
2. *Anthurium crystallinum* (medium)
3. *Schefflera digitata* (*Dizygotheca elegantissima*) (tall)
4. *Adiantum raddianum* (small)

Position shade or brighter indirect light
Temperature 13C (55F) min.; 1 best at 15C (60F) min.; 3 and 4 down to 5C (40F)
Humidity reasonable, especially for 1 and 4
Watering and feeding keep evenly moist in summer, less so in winter. Normal feeding; reduced for 1, see pages 109–110
Comments 1 needs orchid compost, see page 109. Take great care to avoid damaging the young growth of 2.

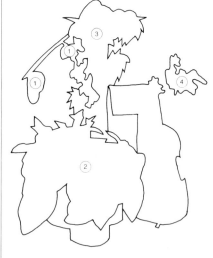

Forest Floor Foliage — Page 84

1. *Spathiphyllum floribundum* (medium, all-year)
2. *Alocasia watsoniana* (medium)
3. *Calathea insignis* (*C. lancifolia*) (medium)

Position subdued light
Temperature 13C (55F) min.
Humidity reasonable, especially at high temperatures
Watering and feeding keep evenly moist in summer, less so in winter. Normal feeding
Comments avoid damaging young growth of 2.

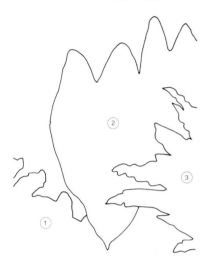

Tropical Evocation — Page 85

1. *Phoenix roebeleii* (tall)
2. *Cycas revoluta* (medium)
3. *Pachypodium lamerei* (medium)
4. *Phoenix canariensis* (tall)
5. *Aloe ferox* (medium)
6. *Yucca elephantipes* (tall)
7. *Washingtonia filifera* (tall)
8. *Brugmansia* (*Datura*) *suaveolens* (tall)

Position several hours of sunshine a day as a minimum; 1, 4, 7 and 6 tolerate good indirect light; 2 tolerates light shade
Temperature min. of just above 0C (32F)
Watering and feeding 8 needs frequent and copious watering in summer, allow to dry out in winter; feed generously with tomato fertilizer in active growth. Allow 3 to dry out before watering in summer; keep more or less dry in winter. Remainder require normal watering and feeding
Comments 8 flowers best in very good light or outside during summer; cut back in autumn by no more than quarter of its height, harder pruning will inhibit flowering.

Magnificent Medinilla — Page 86

Medinilla magnifica

Position good indirect light
Temperature 13C (55F) min.
Humidity reasonable humidity essential
Watering and feeding normal in summer; reduce water in winter
Comments support if necessary.

A Tropical Conservatory — Page 87

1. *Spathiphyllum* 'Mauna Loa' (medium, all-year)
2. *Tillandsia cyanea* (small, all-year)
3. *Dendrobium phalaenopsis* (*D. bigibbum*) (small, spring-autumn)
4. *Philodendron* species (climber)
5. *Phalaenopsis* hybrids (medium, all-year)
6. *Medinilla magnifica* (medium, summer)
7. *Alocasia cuprea* (medium)
8. *Aechmea fasciata* (medium, all-summer)
9. *Fittonia verschaffeltii* (small)
10. *Pellaea rotundifolia* (small)
11. *Davallia* species (small)
12. *Peperomia caperata* (small)
13. *Bougainvillea glabra* (climber, all-year)
14. *Nepenthes* species (medium, all-year)

Position conservatory that receives very little direct sun
Temperature 13C (55F) min.; 5 prefers 10C (60F) min.
Humidity reasonable to high
Watering and feeding these plants are watered with an automatic overhead misting system, as plants grown on branches in this way need constant humidity and moisture. Feed, at half normal strength, is applied similarly
Comments growing epiphytes like orchids and bromeliads on branches like this is great fun, but many need constant moisture which is difficult to achieve unless automated. Plants are attached to the wood with wire, and the orchids are wrapped in a wad of plastic netting to encourage initial rooting.

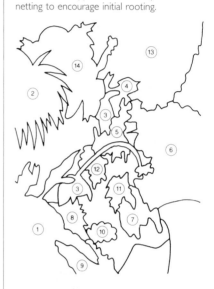

GREEN CASCADES
Climbers and trailers

A Gallery Festooned — Page 88

1. *Neodypsis decaryi* (tall)
2. *Chamaedorea costaricana* (tall)
3. *Ficus benjamina* (tall)
4. *Philodendron domesticum* (*P. hastatum*) (climber)
5. *Begonia* 'Thurstonii' (medium, spring-summer)

Position good indirect light
Temperature 10C (50F) min.; short periods slightly lower won't hurt
Humidity dry air harmful
Watering and feeding normal
Comments 1 is woven through the bars of the gallery.

| Champion Swiss Cheese | Page 90 |

Monstera deliciosa (climber)

Position good indirect light, a few hours of direct sun a day
Temperature 10C (50F) min.
Humidity dry air harmful
Watering and feeding allow to dry out slightly between waterings. Feed conventionally through the compost and via the aerial roots
Comments never cut off aerial roots, but direct back into the compost or into hidden bottles kept full of a diluted nutrient solution. Keep leaves shiny by dusting with a damp cloth when necessary.

| Ferns on the Wall | Page 91 |

1. *Pyrrosia lingua* (small)
2. *Asparagus densiflorus* 'Myersii' (medium)
3. *Drynaria* species (medium)
4. *Platycerium bifurcatum* (medium)

Position shade or soft, indirect light
Temperature 8C (46F) min.
Humidity reasonable
Watering and feeding keep slightly moist in summer; allow to dry out slightly in winter. Feed at half normal strength
Comments ferns, like orchids and bromeliads can be grown on cork or other bark, but keep them and their surrounding atmosphere moist by misting. If they dry out, soak briefly in a bucket of water.

| Self-clinging Creeper | Page 92 |

1. *Aloe* species (medium)
2. *Ficus pumila* (climber)
3. *Aloe ferox* (tall)
4. *Schefflera* (*Heptapleurum*) *arboricola* (tall)

Position good indirect light, although 2 is happy in shade; 1 and 3 are here for winter, being moved onto a sunny terrace in summer

Temperature 8C (46F) min.; 1 and, 3 down to 0C (32F) if kept dry
Humidity 2 reasonable; 1 and 3 tolerant of dry air
Watering and feeding keep 2 constantly moist; water 1 and 3 normally in summer, very little in winter. Normal feeding
Comments allow 2 to trail or climb by means of its stem roots.

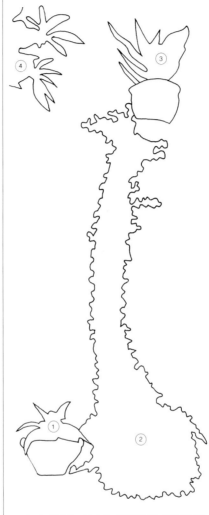

| Filling a Corner | Page 93 |

1. *Scindapsus aureus* (climber)
2. *Saintpaulia* 'Carolina' (small, all-year)
3. *Saintpaulia* 'Wing Song' (small, all-year)
4. *Saintpaulia* 'Skagit's Ambassador' (small, all-year)

Position soft indirect light
Temperature 13C (55F) min.
Humidity dry air harmful
Watering and feeding allow to dry out between waterings; regular use of a proprietary feed will encourage 2, 3 and 4 to flower
Comments 1 often looks best as a trailer, but can be grown up a moss pole, or as here, supported invisibly by pins

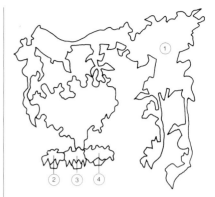

| A Waterfall of Leaves | Page 94 |

From left to right:
Nematanthus 'Black Gold' (medium, late summer-winter)
Columnea unnamed hybrid (medium, late summer-winter)

Position good indirect light
Temperature 10C (50F) min.
Humidity reasonable
Watering and feeding allow to dry out slightly between waterings, especially in winter. Normal feeding.

| Fiery Flowers | Page 95 |

Columnea 'Midnight Lantern' (medium, late summer-winter)

For position and care see above, 'A Waterfall of Leaves'.

| Stairway Bower | Page 96 |

From top to bottom:
1. *Cissus rhombifolia* (climber)
2. *Pteris cretica* (medium)

Position good indirect light to light shade
Temperature 5C (40F) min.
Humidity dry air harmful, especially for the pteris
Watering and feeding normal
Comments *Cissus* climbs by means of tendrils and so will need support, in this case invisible thread and pins; such vigorous growers need occasional pruning.

| Miniature Climber | Page 97 |

From left to right:
1. *Syngonium podophyllum* 'Emerald Gem' (climber)
2. *Peperomia grisoargentea* (small)
3. *Aglaonema* 'Silver Queen' (medium)

Position indirect light or part shade
Temperature 10C (50F) min.
Humidity reasonable

Watering and feeding 1 and 3 need fairly constant moisture in summer; allow to dry out between waterings in winter. Allow 2 to dry between waterings, needs little in winter. Normal feeding
Comments 1 is on a more environmentally responsible equivalent of a moss pole, containing organic fibrous material; encourage the plant to root into the material by spraying it with water.

LIVING ON AIR
Bromeliads – the born survivors

Driftwood Home	Page 98

1. *Tillandsia butzii* (small, all-year)
2. *Tillandsia juncifolia* (small, all-year)
3. *Tillandsia balbisiana* (small, all-year)
4. *Tillandsia tenuifolia* (small, all-year)
5. *Tillandsia oaxacana* (small, all-year)
6. *Tillandsia gardneri* (small, all-year)

Position good indirect light, or with a few hours of sunshine a day
Temperature 5C (40F) min.
Humidity dry air harmful
Watering and feeding mist plants or dunk in water, for details see page 101
Comments wedge plants into crevices in the driftwood, do not glue; no compost required.

Bromeliad Diversity	Page 100

1. *Tillandsia caput-medusae* (small, all-year)
2. *Tillandsia xergraphica* (medium, all-year)
3. *Tillandsia concolor* (small, all-year)
4. *Tillandsia capitata* (small, all-year)
5. *Tillandsia ionantha scaposa* (small, all-year)
6. *Cryptanthus* 'It' (small)

7. *Cryptobergia* species (medium, all-year)
8. *Aechmea fasciata* (medium, all-year)
9. *Billbergia* species (medium, autumn)
10. *Aechmea* 'Bert' (medium, all-year)
11. *Aechmea chantinii* (medium, all-year)
12. *Aechmea fasciata* (medium, all-year)
13. *Aechmea caudata* 'Variegata' (medium, all-year)
14. *Billbergia* × *windii* (medium, autumn)
15. *Billbergia euphemiae* (medium, autumn)

Position good indirect light, or with a few hours of sunshine a day
Temperature 5C (40F) min.
Humidity dry air harmful
Watering and feeding mist 1-6, for details see page 101; 7-13 water through central urn, feed occasionally at half strength; 9, 14 and 15 normal
Comments wedge 1-6 into crevices in the driftwood, do not glue, no compost required; 7, 8, 10, 11, 12 and 13 have small root systems; 7-15 produce offsets; 8 and 12 show the colour variation that often occurs between bromeliads of the same species.

Exotic Colour Splash	Page 101

Aechmea chantinii (medium, all-year)

Position good indirect light
Temperature 10C (50F) min.
Humidity dry air harmful
Watering and feeding water through central urn; feed occasionally at half strength
Comments no need to re-pot as the root system is small; because of this it can be unstable, so support may be necessary.

Billbergia Cascade	Page 102

From top to bottom:
1. *Cissus rhombifolia* (climber)
2. *Billbergia* × *windii* (medium, autumn)

Position several hours of sun a day
Temperature 5C (40F) min.
Humidity dry air harmful
Watering and feeding normal
Comments as with many bromeliads, the old rosettes of 2 die after flowering, leaving younger offsets to gradually fill the pot.

Painted Jungle	Page 103

1. *Aechmea comata* (medium, all-year)
2. *Vriesea splendens* (medium, all-year)
3. *Calathea picturata* 'Vandenheckii' (medium)
4. *Maranta leuconeura* var. *kerchoveana* (small)

Position 1, 2 good indirect light; 3, 4 indirect light or shade
Temperature 10C (50F) min.; 3 needs 13C (55F) min.
Humidity reasonable
Watering and feeding water 1 and 2 only through the urn; feed at half normal strength. 3 and 4 normal.

Air Borne   Page 104

1. *Tillandsia argentea* (small, all-year)
2. *Tillandsia ionantha* (small, all-year)
3. *Tillandsia filifolia* (small, all-year)
4. *Tillandsia butzii* (small, all-year)
5. *Tillandsia pruinosa* (small, all-year)
6. *Tillandsia andreana* (small, all-year)
7. *Tillandsia ionantha scaposa* (small, all-year)

Position good indirect light; a few hours of sunshine a day are acceptable
Temperature 5C (40F) min.
Humidity dry air harmful
Watering and feeding mist plants or dunk in water, for details see pages 101
Comments no need for re-potting! Avoid using aerosols and other domestic sprays.

Bromeliad Tree   Page 105

1. *Tillandsia oaxacana* (small, all-year)
2. *Tillandsia gardneri* (small, all-year)
3. *Tillandsia crocata* (small, all-year)
4. *Tillandsia ionantha* (small, all-year)
5. *Tillandsia andreana* (small, all-year)
6. *Tillandsia ionantha scaposa* (small, all-year)
7. *Tillandsia usneoides* (trailer)
8. *Tillandsia stricta* (small, all-year)

9. *Cryptanthus bivittatus* 'Pink Starlight' (small)
10. *Blechnum gibbum* (medium)
11. *Maranta leuconeura var. erythrophylla* (small)
12. *Alocasia* 'Green Goddess' (medium)
13. *Platycerium grande* (medium)

Position indirect light; 1-9 tolerate a few hours of sunshine a day
Temperature 1-9 5C (40F) min.; 10, 11 and 13 10C (50F) min.; 12 12C (54F) min.
Humidity reasonable
Watering and feeding 1-9 mist plants, for details see page 101; 10-13 normal
Comments 1-9 can live without compost, but need more humid conditions, see page 101.

PERFECTLY SENSUAL
The intriguing orchids

Elegant Intricacy   Page 106

Encyclia cochleata 'Green Octopus' (small, all-year)

Position good indirect light
Temperature 12C (54F)
Humidity reasonable
Watering and feeding see page 109
Comments use orchid compost.

Compact and Colourful   Page 108

1. *Miltonia* Lycaena 'Stamperland' (small, late summer)

2. *Miltonia* Lycaena 'Beall's Strawberry Joy' (small, late summer)
3. *Caladium lindenii* (medium)

Position good indirect light; 3 will tolerate somewhat darker conditions
Temperature 12C (54F) min.
Humidity reasonable
Watering and feeding 3 normal; 1 and 2 see page 109
Comments 1 and 2 need orchid compost.

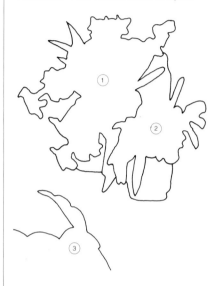

A Sensual Touch   Page 109

From left to right:
Phalaenopsis (Barbara Moler x Carissimo) (medium, all-year)
Doritis pulcherrima (medium, all-year)

Position shade or soft indirect light
Temperature 15C (60F) min.
Humidity reasonable
Watering and feeding see pages 109–110
Comments use orchid compost.

Subtle Style   Page 110

Gongora galatea (small, late summer)

Position good indirect light
Temperature 12C (54F) min.
Humidity reasonable
Watering and feeding see page 109
Comments use orchid compost.

The Classic Orchid   Page 111

x *Laeliocattleya* Elizabeth Fulton (small, autumn)

For position and care see above, 'Subtle Style'.

An Oriental Touch — *Page 112*

1. *Miltoniopsis* 'Strawberry Joy' (small, late summer)
2. *Miltonia Anjou* 'St. Patrick' (small, late summer)
3. *Miltoniopsis* 'Alexander Dumas' (small, late summer)
4. *Begonia* 'Cleopatra'

For position and care of 1, 2, 3 see above, 'Subtle Style'.
Watering and feeding 4 normal.

The Phalaenopsis Paintbox — *Page 113*

1. *Phalaenopsis* Elise de Valee (medium, all-year)
2. *Phalaenopsis* (Alide × Satin Silk) (medium, all-year)
3. *Phalaenopsis* (Golden Buddha × Smartissimo) (medium, all-year)
4. *Phalaenopsis* Redfan (medium, all-year)
5. *Phalaenopsis* Pink Pride (medium, all-year)
6. *Phalaenopsis* (Danse × Matapi) (medium, all-year)
7. *Phalaenopsis* (Capella × Chardonneret) (medium, all-year)
8. *Phalaenopsis* Cacharel Roc (medium, all-year)
9. *Phalaenopsis* Mira Golden (medium, all-year)

Position soft indirect light
Temperature 15C (60F) min.
Humidity reasonable
Watering and feeding see pages 109–110
Comments use orchid compost.

Dining with Company — *Page 114*

1. *Miltoniopsis roezii* 'Alba' (small, late summer)
2. *Coelogyne mooreana* 'Brockhurst' (small, late summer)
3. *Gongora galatea* (small, late summer)
4. *Encyclia cochleata* 'Green Octopus' (small, all-year)
5. *Brassia verrucosa* (medium, summer-autumn)
6. × *Laeliocattleya* 'Elizabeth Fulton' (small, autumn)
7. *Howea forsteriana* (tall)

Position a temporary display for flowers; all do well in good indirect light; 7 does well in shade
Temperature 12C (54F) min.; 2, 5 and 7 down to 10C (50F)
Humidity reasonable
Watering and feeding 7 normal in summer, less in winter; 1 to 6 see page 109
Comments repot 1 to 6 in orchid compost.

Heavenly Scent — *Page 115*

Brassia verrucosa (medium, autumn)

Position good indirect light
Temperature 10C (50F) min.
Humidity reasonable
Watering and feeding see page 109
Comments use orchid compost.

Forest Floor Beauty — *Page 116*

Paphiopedilum hybrid (small, winter)

Position soft indirect light
Temperature 12C (54F) min.
Humidity reasonable
Watering and feeding see pages 109 and 111
Comments use orchid compost.

Pure as Driven Snow — *Page 117*

Phalaenopsis hybrids (medium, all-year)

Position indirect light
Temperature 15C (60F) min.
Humidity reasonable
Watering and feeding see pages 109–110
Comments use orchid compost.

A WORLD APART
Making the most of conservatories

Basking Under Glass — *Page 118*

1. *Lilium* 'Destiny' (medium, early summer)
2. *Fuchsia* cultivar (medium, all-summer)
3. *Abutilon* 'Canary Bird' (tall, spring-autumn)
4. *Argyranthemum* hybrid (medium, summer)
5. *Nerium oleander* 'Tito Poggi' (tall, summer-autumn)
6. *Nerium oleander* 'Jannoch' (tall, summer-autumn)
7. *Pelargonium* cultivars (medium, summer)
8. *Jasminum polyanthum* (climber, winter)

Position direct sunlight as much as possible
Temperature -2C (28F) min.
Humidity average
Watering and feeding generous in summer; keep drier and stop feeding in winter
Comments plant 1 deeply in tall pots and do not neglect after flowering. Cut back 3, 5 and 6 in autumn if they become too tall; they will re-sprout even if cut to ground level. For pests and diseases, see page 136.

Exploiting the Space
Page 120

1. *Tradescantia* species (small)
2. Zonal pelargonium (medium, all-year)

3. *Lotus bertholettii* (medium, early summer)
4. *Tradescantia pallida* (Setcreasea purpurea) (medium, summer)
5. *Lotus x maculatus* (medium, all-year)
6. *Pelargonium* Balcon Series (trailer, all-year)
7. *Lapageria rosea* (climber, autumn)
8. *Abutilon* cultivar (tall, spring-autumn)
9. *Abutilon pictum* 'Thompsonii' (tall, spring-autumn)
10. *Brugmansia (Datura) suaveolens rosea* (tall, summer-autumn)
11. *Polygala x dalmaisiana* (*P. myrtifolia* 'Grandiflora') (medium, spring-autumn)
12. *Melaleuca thymifolia* (medium, summer)

Position direct sun for at least half the day
Temperature 0C (32F) min.
Humidity average
Watering and feeding generously in summer; keep drier and stop feeding in winter
Comments for pruning 8 and 9, see comments for page 118 'Basking Under Glass'; 10 should not be cut back too hard; others will require minimal pruning. For pests and diseases see page 136.

Shelves of Flower
Page 121

1. *Chlorophytum comosum* 'Vittatum' (medium)
2. Zonal pelargoniums (medium, all-year)
3. *Campanula isophylla* 'Mayi' (small, spring-autumn)

4. *Argyranthemum* 'Petite Pink' (small, spring-autumn)
5. *Schefflera (Heptapleurum) arboricola* (tall)
6. *Argyranthemum* 'Jamaica Primrose' (medium, spring-autumn)
7. *Brachycome iberidifolia* (small, summer)
8. *Hedera helix* ssp. *helix* cultivars (climbers)
9. *Solenostemon (Coleus)* cultivar (medium)
10. *Jasminum polyanthum* (climber, winter)

Position direct sun for at least half the day; 5 tolerates indirect light; 1 and 8 tolerate soft light
Temperature 0C (32F) min.; 5 needs 5C (40F)
Humidity average
Watering and feeding generously in summer; keep drier and stop feeding in winter
Comments cut back if necessary in autumn. For pests and diseases see page 136.

Flying Saucers
Page 122

From left to right:
1. *Pelargonium* cultivars (medium, summer)
2. *Pelargonium graveolens* (medium, summer)
3. *Pelargonium tomentosum* (medium, summer)
4. *Pelargonium* cultivar (medium, summer)

Position sun for at least half the day
Temperature 0C (32F) min.
Humidity average
Watering and feeding plentiful in summer; keep almost dry and no feeding in winter, especially if the plants kept cool

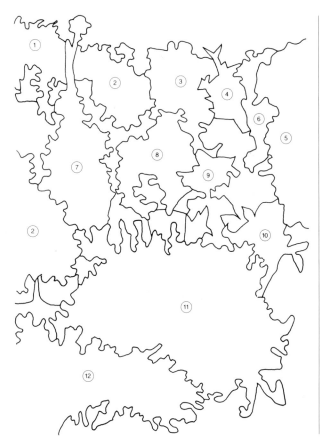

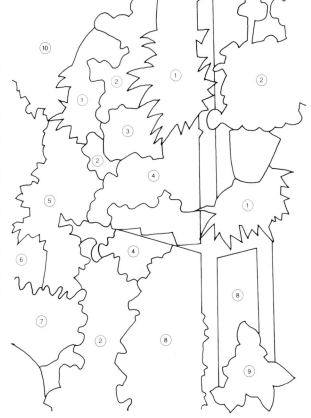

Comments cut back in autumn. Pelargoniums are susceptible to botrytis (grey mould) in winter when ventilation, careful watering and removal of dead leaves and flowers are needed. For pests and diseases see page 136.

Once a Station Platform   Page 123

1. *Bougainvillea glabra* (climber, all-year)
2. *Plumbago auriculata* (climber, summer)
3. *Plumbago auriculata* var. *alba* (climber, summer)
4. *Billbergia × windii* (medium, summer)
5. *Begonia bowerae* (medium)
6. *Cordyline fruticosa* 'Red Edge' (medium)
7. *Streptocarpus saxorum* (medium, summer)
8. *Crassula ovata* (*C. argentea*) (medium)
9. *Sedum sieboldii* (small, late summer)
10. *Neoregelia carolinae* forma *tricolor* (medium, all-year)
11. *Cycas revoluta* (medium)
12. *Passiflora racemosa* (climber, summer)

Position as much sun as possible for 1, 2, 3, 8, 9 and 12; good indirect light for 4, 5, 6, 7, 10
Temperature 9 is hardy; 1, 2, 3, 11, 12 0C (32F) min.; 4, 5, 6, 7, 8 and 10 8C (46F) min.
Humidity reasonable
Watering and feeding normal; 1, 2, 3 and 12 generous in summer; 10 water and feed at half strength into urn
Comments cut climbers back if necessary in autumn. For pests and diseases see page 136.

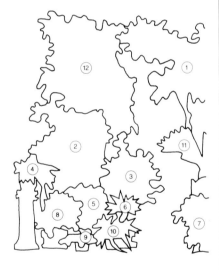

One's Own Jungle   Page 124

1. *Tillandsia usneoides* (trailer)
2. *Stanhopea tigrina* (medium, summer)
3. *Gloriosa superba* 'Rothschildiana' (climber, summer)
4. *Plumbago auriculata* (climber, summer)
5. *Sedum morganianum* (medium)
6. *Humea elegans* (medium, summer)

Position sun for no more than half the day; 4 and 5 prefer more

Temperature 10C (50F) min.; 1 down to 5C (40F); 4 0C (32F) min.
Humidity reasonable
Watering and feeding 1, an air plant, needs misting; treat 2 as other orchids with pseudobulbs, see page 109; feed and water 3 generously in summer and dry off in winter; 4 treat generously; keep 5 dry in winter; 6 normal
Comments 3 dies back to a tuber in the winter which should be kept dry until spring, then start back into growth in a warm place. Grow 2 in orchid compost in a basket rather than a pot, or the flower will grow down into the compost. Try and save seed from 6 to sow

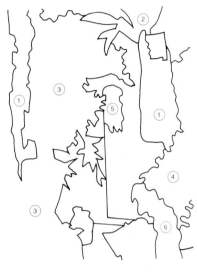

the following year, as it is a biennial. For pests and diseases see page 136.

Face the Setting Sun   Page 125

1. *Cycas revoluta* (medium)
2. *Abutilon* 'Cannington Carol' (medium, summer)
3. Zonal pelargoniums (medium, all-year)
4. *Crassula* species (medium)
5. *Dracaena marginata* 'Tricolor' (medium)
6. *Pelargonium* 'Blakesdorf' (small, summer)
7. *Solenostemon* (*Coleus*) cultivars (medium)
8. *Chlorophytum comosum* 'Vittatum' (medium)
9. *Argyranthemum frutescens* (medium, summer-autumn)
10. *Hedera helix* ssp. *helix* cultivar (climber)

Position direct sun for at least half the day; 1, 5, 7, 8, 10 tolerate softer light
Temperature 0C (32F) min.; 5, 6 and 7 safer at 5C (40F) min.
Humidity average
Watering and feeding generous in summer, reduce in winter
Comments cut back in autumn if required.

Plenty to Look at   Page 127

1. *Yucca elephantipes* (tall)
2. *Abutilon* 'Savitzii' (tall, summer)
3. *Cordyline australis* (tall)
4. *Spathiphyllum* 'Mauna Loa' (medium)
5. *Polystichium setiferum* (medium)
6. *Tradescantia pallida* (*Setcreasea purpurea*) (medium, summer)
7. *Passiflora racemosa* (climber, summer)
8. *Davallia trichomanoides* (small)
9. *Plumbago auriculata* (climber, summer)
10. *Nephrolepis exaltata* (medium)
11. *Streptocarpus* hybrid (small, summer)
12. *Philodendron erubescens* 'Burgundy' (climber)
13. *Musa velutina* (tall)
14. *Adiantum raddianum* (small)
15. *Asplenium nidus* (medium)
16. *Begonia bowerae* (small)
17. *Crassula ovata* (*C. argentea*) (medium)
18. *Blechnum gibbum* (medium)
19. *Pelargonium* cultivar (medium, summer)
20. *Bougainvillea spectabilis* (climber, summer)

Position as much sun as possible for 1, 2, 3, 6, 7, 9, 13 and 17; remainder, on the left, prefer more indirect light
Temperature 10C (50F) min.; 3 and 5 are hardy; 1, 2, 6, 7, 8, 17 down to 0C (32F); 10 and 11 to 5C (40F)
Humidity reasonable
Watering and feeding plentiful water and normal feeding in growth; feed and water 2, 7 and 9 generously in summer; keep them all drier in winter

Dine in Style   Page 126

1. *Plumbago auriculata* (climber, summer)
2. *Plumbago auriculata* var. *alba* (climber, summer)
3. *Passiflora racemosa* (climber, summer)
4. *Tradescantia pallida* (*Setcreasea purpurea*) (medium, summer)
5. *Adiantum raddianum* (small)
6. *Abutilon* 'Savitzii' (tall, summer)
7. *Pelargonium* hybrids (medium, summer)
8. *Cycas revoluta* (medium)
9. *Spathiphyllum* 'Mauna Loa' (medium)
10. *Blechnum gibbum* (medium)
11. *Aspidistra elatior* 'Variegata' (medium)
12. *Erythrina crista-galli* (medium, summer)
13. *Begonia bowerae* (small)
14. *Cordyline fruticosa* 'Red Edge' (medium)

Position as much sun as possible for 1, 2, 3, 4, 6, 7, 10; more indirect light for the others
Temperature 10C (50F) min.; 1, 2, 3, 4, 5, 6, 8, 10, 11 down to 0C (32F)
Humidity average; 5, 9 and 12 reasonable
Watering and feeding be generous with 1, 2, 3 and 6 during summer; remainder need plentiful water but normal feeding in growth but keep drier in winter
Comments cut back 1, 2, 3 and 6, hard if necessary, in autumn. For pests and diseases see page 136.

Comments cut back 2, 7 and 9, hard if necessary, in autumn. For pests and diseases see page 136.

| Miniature Mediterranean | Page 128 |

1. *Trachycarpus fortunei* (tall)
2. *Citrus* cultivars (tall, winter)
3. *Euphorbia tirucalli* (tall)
4. *Nerium oleander* 'Tito Poggi' (tall, summer-autumn)
5. *Bougainvillea glabra* (climber, all-year)
6. *Chrysalidocarpus lutescens* (tall)
7. *Pelargonium* 'Tip Top Duet' (small, summer)
8. *Pelargonium* 'Catford Belle' (small, summer)
9. *Streptocarpus* hybrid (small, summer)
10. *Cycas revoluta* (medium)
11. *Begonia haageana* (*B. scharffii*) (medium, summer)
12. *Araucaria heterophylla* (tall)

Position as much sun as possible; 1, 6, 9, 10 and 11 prefer good indirect light
Temperature 5C (40F) min.; 6 and 11 10C (50F) min.; 1 is hardy
Humidity average
Watering and feeding generous in summer; reduce in winter

Comments watch out for scale on 2, also yellowing leaves, a sign of mineral deficiencies which can be cured with a trace element tonic. For other pests and diseases see page 136.

| The View at the Deep End | Page 129 |

1. *Euphorbia tirucalli* (tall)
2. *Yucca elephantipes* (tall)
3. *Araucaria heterophylla* (tall)
4. *Trachycarpus fortunei* (tall)
5. *Cocos nucifera* (medium)
6. *Musa* species (tall)

Position direct sun for at least half the day
Temperature 5C (40F) min.; 5 and 6 10C (50F) min.
Humidity reasonable
Watering and feeding normal
Comments the remarkably small pots are possible because the plants are growing 'hydroponically', a special technique which involves using inert granules instead of soil and constant liquid feeding. *Cocos* (coconut) will not survive for any length of time.

| Always Colourful | Page 130 |

1. *Nerium oleander* 'Tito Poggii' (tall, summer-autumn)
2. *Passiflora racemosa* (climber, summer)
3. *Plumbago auriculata* (climber, summer)
4. Zonal pelargoniums F1 hybrids (medium, summer)
5. *Crassula ovata* (medium)
6. *Pteris cretica* 'Alexandrae' (small)

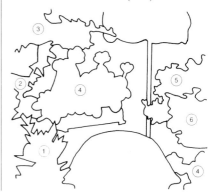

Position full sun for at least half the day except 6 which prefers shade
Temperature -2C (28F) min.; 5 and 6 0C (32F) min.
Humidity average
Watering and feeding water and feed well in summer; keep drier and cease feeding in winter; 6 needs constant moisture
Comments in autumn cut back 2, 3 and 4, and any leggy stems of 1. For pests and diseases, see page 136

Flourishing Vine	Page 131

1. Grape vine (climber, fruiting)
2. *Solanum rantonnettii* (tall, summer-autumn)
3. *Nerium oleander* 'Emile Sahut' (tall, summer-autumn)
4. Zonal pelargonium hybrids (small, summer)
5. *Salvia patens* (medium, summer-autumn)
6. *Sollya heterophylla* (climber, summer)
7. *Abutilon* species (tall, summer)
8. *Nerium oleander* 'Marie Gambetta' (tall, summer-autumn)
9. *Freesia* hybrid (medium, spring-summer)

Position direct sun for at least half the day
Temperature -2C (28F) min.
Humidity average
Watering and feeding generous in summer; keep drier and cease feeding in winter
Comments in autumn cut back 1 hard and any leggy stems of 3 and 8; 5 dies down over the winter. For pests and diseases, see page 137.

Tropical Comfort	Page 132

1. *Citrus x paradisii* 'Red Blush' (tall, winter)
2. *Anthurium andreanum* (medium, all-year)
3. *Calathea zebrina* (medium)
4. *Acalypha wilkesiana* (tall)
5. *Asplenium nidus* (medium)

Position indirect light
Temperature 12C (54F) min.; 1 down to 5C (40F) min.
Humidity reasonable
Watering and feeding generous in summer; dry out a little before watering in winter. Normal feeding
Comments stand 1 outside in summer, bring in before the first frost to flower during the winter.

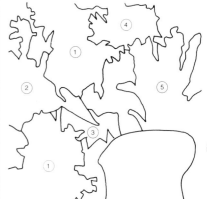

FURTHER READING

A to Z guides
Among the best are:

Davidson, W. *Unusual House Plants: The Easy Guide to Buying and Growing Spectacular Varieties.* London: Ward Lock, 1990; pbk 1992.
For the more adventurous.

Herwig, R and Schubert, M. *The Complete Book of House Plants.* Cambridge: Lutterworth Press, 2nd revised edition 1991.

Hessayon, D G. *The New House Plant Expert.* London: Expert Books, 1991. New York: Sterling Publishing Co, 1990. Very good detailed advice.

Ledward, D. *Homing in on House Plants.* London: Robson Books, pbk, 1992. Down-to-earth and realistic approach.

Reader's Digest Success with House Plants. London and New York: Reader's Digest, 1980. Among the most detailed on the subject.

Bonsai
Pike, D. *Indoor Bonsai.* Marlborough, England: Crowood Press, 1989. Distributed in USA by Trafalgar House.

Bromeliads
Rauh, W: *Bromeliad Lexicon.* London: Blandford Press, revised edition 1991. New York: Sterling Publishing Co, 1990.

Orchids
MacKenzie Black, Peter: *The Complete Book of Orchid Growing.* London: Ward Lock, 1981. Vermont: Trafalgar, 1988. Good on basic cultivations, but only covers species.

Rittershausen, B and W: *Orchid Growing Illustrated.* London: Blandford Press, 1993. New York: Sterling Publishing Co, 1985.

Rittershausen, W: *Step by Step Guide to Growing and Displaying Orchids.* Eastbourne, England: Gardner's Books, 1993.

PERIODICALS

HousePlant: a stimulating quarterly magazine and excellent source for nurseries, products and specialists societies. Enquiries to PO Box 1638, Elkins, West Virginia 26241-9910. (304) 636 1212.

SOCIETIES

Great Britain
The Orchid Society of Great Britain
Athelney, 145 Binscombe Village, Goldalming, Surrey GU7 3QL

Saintpaulia and House Plant Society
33 Common Road
Langley, Slough SL3 8JZ

North America
See also *HousePlant magazine*.

American Gesneriad Society
88 Maynard Street
Roslingdale MA 02131

American Orchid Society
60005 Olive Avenue
West Palm Beach FL 33405
(407) 585 8666

LIST OF SUPPLIERS

Please note: names, addresses and telephone numbers were correct at the time this book went to press. It is advisable to telephone in advance to check opening times.

NURSERIES

Great Britain
Bloomsbury
Upper Lodge Farm
Padworth Common
Berkshire RH7 4JD
0734 700239
Conservatory plants and unusual hardy plants

Mail order and retail
Send 5 first class stamps for a catalogue

Burnham Nurseries
Forches Cross, Newton Abbot
Devon TQ12 6BZ
0626 52233
Orchids
Mail order and retail
Send sae for a catalogue

Dibley's Nurseries
Llanelidan, Ruthin
Clwyd LL15 2LG
0978 790677
Gesneriads, including streptocarpus; also begonias
Mail order and retail
Send sae for a catalogue

Brian Hiley
25 Little Woodcote Estate
Wallington, Surrey SM5 4AU
081-647 9679
Conservatory plants
Mail order and retail
Send 3 first class stamps for a catalogue

Newington Nursery
Bathway Farm
Tewton Mendip
Somerset BA3 4LN
0761 241283
Conservatory and sub-tropical plants
Mail order and retail
Catalogue £1.75

The Palm Centre
563 Upper Richmond Road
West, London SW14 7ED
081-876 1193
(fax 081-876 6888)
Palms, cycads, bamboos and other exotics
Catalogue for palms and cycads £1.95

Reads Nursery
Halles Hall, Loddon
Norfolk NR14 6QW
0508 548 395
Conservatory plants, citrus
Mail order and retail
Send 4 first class stamps for a catalogue

Special Plants
Laurels Farm, Upper Wraxall
nr Chippenham, SN14 7AG
0225 891686

Conservatory and unusual patio plants
Retail only
Send 4 first class stamps for a catalogue

Tropical Rain Forest
66 Castle Grove Avenue
Leeds LS6 4BS
0532 789810
Air plants
Mail order only, no visitors
Send 3 first class stamps for a catalogue

Tropicana Nursery
Westhill Avenue
Torquay, Devon TQ1 4LH
0803 312618
Conservatory and sub-tropical plants
Mail order and retail
Send 4 first class stamps for catalogue
Colour brochure £1.75

Wyld Court Rainforest
Hampstead Norreys, Newbury, Berkshire RG16 0TN
0635 200221
Tropical plants
Retail
Tropical botanical garden open all year except Xmas Day and Boxing Day

BIOLOGICAL CONTROL

Defenders Ltd
PO Box 131
Wye, Kent TN25 5TQ

Natural Pest Control
Yapton Road, Barnhaven
Bognor Regis, West Sussex
PO22 0BQ

Wyebugs
Department of Biological Sciences, Wye College, Ashford, Kent TN25 5AH

NURSERIES

North America
Glasshouse Works Greenhouses
Church Street, PO Box 97, Stewart, Ohio 45778-0097
(614) 662 2142

Tropical and subtropical, distinctive and variegated plants
Mail order and retail

The Grassroots Garden
131 Spring Street
New York 10012
(212) 226 2662
Sculptural plants
Mail order and retail

Logees Glasshouses
141 North Street,
Danielson CT 06239,
(203) 774 8038
Tropical and conservatory plants
Mail order and retail

J & L Orchids
20 Sherwood Road
Easton, Connecticut 06612
(203) 261 3772
Cool growing, miniature orchids
Mail order and retail

Orchid World International Inc,
10885 SW 95th Street
Miami, Florida 33176
(305) 271 0268
Tropical orchids
Mail order and retail

Stewart Orchids
PO Box 550
3376 Foothill Road
Carpinteria, California
(805) 684 5448
Cattleyas and temperature orchids
Mail order and retail

INDEX

Please note: references in *italics* denote illustrations; plants in Key to Plant Information pages 137–155 are not indexed.

ACKNOWLEDGEMENTS

I am indebted to numerous people who helped me with this book: commercial growers, amateur indoor plant enthusiasts and those who allowed Jerry and myself to turn their homes upside down while we carted plants in and out. Especial thanks to those who actually offered us hospitality while we rearranged their furniture and possessions! I am grateful to Nick Rigdon and the staff at Cannington College, Somerset, and Nick Wray, at the University of Bristol Botanical Gardens, who loaned us some magnificent plants and all the growers whose establishments are listed on page 157.

For so generously allowing us to use their homes for location or for lending us additional plants, I wish to thank: Diana Wells, Jeremy Walsh, Caroline Tisdall, Tor and Don Foster, Gilda Baikovitch and Graham Fisher, Jan Sawyer, Helen Tann and Pete Maxse, John Cook, Betty and Tony Bradshaw, Teresa Thornhill, Christopher and Val Bradshaw, Lesley and John Jenkins, Pepe and Vernon Stratton, Jonathan and Mary Janson, Nicolas and Maggie Gundry, Helinka Fuglewicz, Stuart Rodger, Stevie West, Derry Watkins, Jason Payne and Pat Cunningham. In New York I would like to thank the following for their help in finding and allowing us to use plants and locations: Linda Yang, Patti Hagan, Edith Chang, Anneli Kaijas-Lundstrom, Ken Druse, Larry Hodgson, Larry Nathanson, Tim du Val, Adam, Victor Nelson and Audrey Eiber.

Many containers were loaned by Dibco of Sevenoaks, Kent. The following helped in carting plants and gear – life would have been very much more difficult without you: Ed Grigg, Robert Morris, Tina (in Brooklyn), Kieran Bradshaw, Fran Forrest and Stewart Taylor. Finally, my thanks to Jo Eliot for her constant love and support.

Picture credits: Bridgeman Art Library 14, 15; Mary Evans Picture Library 10, 16; The Royal Horticultural Society, Lindley Library 9, 11, 13. All other photographs are by Jerry Harpur.

Editorial Director Ian Jackson
Editor Barbara Haynes
Proof Reader Nicky Twyman
Indexer Dorothy Frame
Art Director Elaine Partington
Designer Karen Watts
Line-drawing Artist Anthony Duke
Production Hazel Kirkman and Charles James